Armoured Horseman

Previously Published Books by Peter Willett:

An Introduction to the Thoroughbred (Stanley Paul, 1966)
Five Times Champion (Pelham Books, 1968)
The Thoroughbred (Weidenfeld & Nicolson, 1970)
The Classic Racehorse (Stanley Paul, 1981)
Makers of the Modern Thoroughbred (Century Hutchinson, 1986)
The Story of Tattersalls (Stanley Paul, 1987)
A History of the General Stud Book (Weatherbys, 1991)
Dick Hern (Hodder & Stoughton, 2000)

Armoured Horseman

With The Bays and Eighth Army in North Africa and Italy

Peter Willett

Pen & Sword
MILITARY

First published in Great Britain in 2015 by
Pen & Sword Military
an imprint of
Pen & Sword Books Ltd
47 Church Street
Barnsley
South Yorkshire
S70 2AS

Copyright © Peter Willett 2015

ISBN 978 1 47383 421 7

Typeset in Ehrhardt by
Mac Style Ltd, Bridlington, East Yorkshire
Printed and bound in the UK by CPI Group (UK) Ltd,
Croydon, CRO 4YY

Pen & Sword Books Ltd incorporates the imprints of Pen & Sword
Archaeology, Atlas, Aviation, Battleground, Discovery, Family
History, History, Maritime, Military, Naval, Politics, Railways, Select,
Transport, True Crime, and Fiction, Frontline Books, Leo Cooper,
Praetorian Press, Seaforth Publishing and Wharncliffe.

For a complete list of Pen & Sword titles please contact
PEN & SWORD BOOKS LIMITED
47 Church Street, Barnsley, South Yorkshire, S70 2AS, England
E-mail: enquiries@pen-and-sword.co.uk
Website: www.pen-and-sword.co.uk

Contents

List of Maps

Introduction

I served as an officer in The Queen's Bays (2nd Dragoon Guards) from June 1941 until September 1946 – not long enough to earn the veteran's soubriquet of a 'bloody good old Bay' but not bad for a temporary officer in a regular regiment.

The Bays, as they were commonly known for short, were one of the oldest cavalry regiments. They were formed by James II in 1685, but changed sides and fought in the army of William III at the Battle of the Boyne five years later when James's forces were defeated. They took part in many of the major campaigns of the next two centuries, but missed Waterloo, when they were stationed in Scotland. They fought as infantry on the Western Front at times during the Great War, distinguishing themselves particularly at the Second Battle of Ypres in 1915. They were back on their horses for most of the time between the two world wars, where they excelled at mounted sports and various military competitions. In 1931 they won the Inter-Regimental Polo Tournament at Hurlingham for the first time. The team consisted of George and Evelyn Fanshawe, Tom Draffen and Alex Barclay, all of whom afterwards commanded the regiment, the two last-named being my first two commanding officers. Mechanization began in 1935, but it was not until three years later that the regiment was able to turn out in full strength as an armoured regiment. Equipped with wretchedly inadequate cruiser and light tanks, the regiment fought rearguard actions in the later stages of the Dunkirk campaign before being evacuated from Brest in the middle of June. After several moves they arrived in Marlborough at the beginning of June 1941, and I joined them there two weeks later.

In the Second World War an armoured regiment such as The Queen's Bays consisted for battle purposes of a regimental headquarters of four tanks, and three squadrons, each comprising a headquarters of four tanks and four troops of three tanks each. The regiment was commanded by a lieutenant colonel, each squadron by a major with a captain as second in command, and each troop by a lieutenant or second lieutenant. In addition there was a headquarters squadron comprising all the administrative and supply elements necessary to sustain a regiment in the field. In practice the regiment seldom entered a battle at full strength because the numbers were almost invariably reduced by preliminary actions, breakdowns and lost tracks. For example, B Squadron was launched into the notorious Point 153 attack in September 1944 with no more than four tanks.

Casualties in armoured regiments were light compared with the wholesale slaughter of the infantry in the trenches of the Western Front in the Great War. The battle of Montecieco, which included the attack on Point 153, was the Bays' costliest day of the war, but the regiment suffered only sixty-four casualties (killed and wounded) altogether, including five officers and thirteen other ranks killed. The regiment's casualties in the much longer battles of the Gazala Line and Second Alamein barely exceeded a hundred. Nevertheless, these casualty rates have to be seen in perspective. The tank crews of a squadron at full strength numbered no more than sixty-four, so a small number of casualties drastically reduced a squadron's fighting strength. Moreover, it was rare for the whole crew of a knocked-out tank to be casualties (killed or wounded), but the survivors were eliminated from the battle until a fresh tank could be provided for them. That might take hours or days.

The casualty list at Point 153 provided one remarkable, and tragic, example of the contrary fortunes of war. Captain John McVail had been the principal architect of the astonishing escape of five members of C Squadron from behind the German lines on the Coriano ridge two weeks earlier, but he was killed at Montecieco. In the meantime he had found time to write a 3,000-word account of the exploit, which was printed in Major General Beddington's *History of The Queen's Bays*, in spite of the fraught circumstances of taking over fresh tanks and the move forward over rough countryside and rutted dust-laden tracks. It was an astonishing achievement. A précis of his account is included later in this book.

I count myself very lucky to have served so long in The Queen's Bays. In the ranks of training regiments, and indeed Sandhurst, I had been alone, isolated and unprotected, with nobody to appeal to in case of trouble or injustice. But once established in a good regiment I was accepted as a member of a family and could count on advice and support whatever the circumstances and however blameworthy I might be. For my three commanding officers, Tom Draffen, Alex Barclay, and Daniel Asquith, who embodied that family feeling, I have nothing but affection and respect. In 1959 the regiment amalgamated with the King's Dragoon Guards, and the joint regiment became The Queen's Dragoon Guards (QDGs).

Author's Note

In the chapter 'In the Ranks' there is frequent incidence of the soldier's vernacular used for emphasis. I have renounced the mealy-mouthed evasions of blanks and asterisks because all they do is draw attention to the fact that the writer is straying into forbidden semantic territory. In any case the reader knows perfectly well what the blanks and asterisks stand for. In the soldier's vocabulary the 'F' word has no crude or sexual connotation. It occurs as naturally as, say, 'damn' in the mouths of educated speakers. So I see no valid reason at all for artificial restraint in recording the utterances of my comrades in the ranks.

Acknowledgements

Although this book is based on my personal recollections of events many decades ago, it could never have come to fulfilment without the generous help of many individuals in the recent past. I wish to record my deep gratitude to: Brigadier Henry Wilson, the Publishing Manager of Pen and Sword, without whose constant advice and encouragement the book would never have got off the ground; my editor Richard Doherty, a truly professional military historian, for correcting many crass errors and for his essential contribution to maps and illustrations; the late Mike Tomkin for a graphic account of the opening phase of the second battle of El Alamein; to Major General Robert Ward for the gift of a very special photograph; Brigadier George Powell for invaluable documents relating to the Battle of the Gazala Line; Lieutenant Colonel 'Basher' Brace for great support from Home HQ 1st The Queen's Dragoon Guards; the Regiment for permission to reproduce Joan Wanklyn's painting of an incident at the Gazala Line; Lady Stanier for permission to quote from the privately published autobiography of Field Marshal Sir John Stanier; to Rupert Mackeson of Marlborough Sporting for his confident support; and Katharine Hipwell for her indispensable secretarial work.

Peter Willett
March 2015

Chapter One

Service Tradition in the Family

Thucydides wrote: 'These men were worthy of their country. And you who are left may pray for a more peaceful end. Day by day contemplate your country's power till you grow full of passionate love for her. And when you realize her greatness, remember that it was the dead who won it for you.'

The great Athenian's insistence on honouring the legacy of the dead may have rung true in the fifth century BC and the times of the Peloponnesian War between Athens and Sparta, and indeed for many subsequent centuries, but doubts about its credibility creep in when the twentieth century is reached. Could the mass slaughters on the battle fronts of the Great War really be condoned by the blessings of the eventual peace? There is some evidence that these doubts existed in the minds even of those least likely to harbour them. The message sent by King George V to Field Marshal Sir Douglas Haig, the Commander-in-Chief of the British Armies in France, a week after the signing of the armistice that brought the war to end in November 1918, and distributed to all ranks, had this concluding sentence:

I desire to thank every officer, soldier and woman of our army for services nobly rendered, for sacrifices cheerfully given, and I pray that God, who has been pleased to grant a victorious end to the great crusade for justice and right, will prosper and bless our efforts in the immediate future to secure for generations to come the hard-won blessings of freedom and peace.

The message contained no mention of debt owed to the dead which, in the circumstances, might have seemed heartless and cynical to many of the bereaved families, for example families like that of my maternal grandparents James Wilfred and Cecil Stirling. Their three sons who attained adulthood (a fourth son died of meningitis in infancy) were all killed in action in the Great War. The oldest, Wilfred, was navigating officer of the cruiser HMS *Monmouth* sunk in an attack on a superior German squadron at the Battle of Coronel off the coast of Chile in November 1914. The second, Jack, was in the Cameronians (Scottish Rifles) on the Western Front and was shot by a German sniper when standing on the parapet of a trench directing repairs on 1 January 1915. The youngest, Colin, also was in the Cameronians, but was commanding a battalion of the Royal Berkshire Regiment at Chaunes when he was mortally wounded on 24 March 1918. A lieutenant colonel at the early age of twenty-four, he was an officer of extreme gallantry awarded the MC and DSO and Bar, and four Mentions in Despatches. He died in the Red Cross Hospital at Rouen two months after he was wounded. It is inconceivable that his parents, leaving the hospital after visiting their dying son, would have consoled themselves with the thought that his death, and the deaths of Wilfred and Jack, had ensured the blessings of peace and freedom of future generations of the British people. Such a thought would have been beyond the bounds of bitterest irony.

The only children of James Wilfred and Cecil Stirling to survive their parents were my mother Agnes Mary, known as Nita, and her younger sister Kathleen, known as Kay. Kay's son Michael Turner joined the Cameronians and was killed during the retreat to Dunkirk in 1940.

James Wilfred Stirling, the head of this tragic family, was a soldier of considerable distinction. He was commissioned in the Royal Artillery in 1874 and served for thirty-one years in many different stations at home and abroad, retiring as a colonel in 1905. On the outbreak of the Great War he volunteered to rejoin, offering his services in any capacity though he was fifty-nine years old. He served in France for nearly four years, commanding successively the artillery of the 15th Scottish Division, a

Canadian division and the 59th Division at the major battles of Loos, the Somme, Vimy Ridge and Passchendaele. His obituary in the Royal Artillery Institution papers contained this tribute. 'He was beloved by all who served with him, to whom he set an example of the best qualities of an officer and a gentleman. His devotion to duty, kindness to all and his noble character upheld the best traditions of the Regiment.' His retirement as a brigadier general soon after the death of Colin in 1918 hints at a mental state of anguish and disillusionment, and an urgent wish to be with, and comfort, his heartbroken wife.

My father, Kingsley Willett, also was a regular officer in the Royal Artillery. In 1903 he was posted as a second lieutenant to Exeter, where he was under the command of James Wilfred Stirling and became engaged to Nita Stirling. A keen hunting and steeplechasing man, he rode in races over fences at the small West Country meetings like Totnes, where the runners had to ford the river Dart, a hazard not found on modern racecourses; and in 1904 he won the Royal Artillery Gold Cup at Aldershot on his own mare Cannonesse II. He resigned from the Army in the following year to take charge of the family business, the West Street Brewery in Brighton, which was ailing due to the incompetent management of his father, Percy Arnold Willett. He and Nita were married two years later.

He remained on the Reserve when he left the Army and was called up in the autumn of 1914 soon after the outbreak of the Great War. He served in the Salonika campaign of 1915 before being invalided home with a severe attack of paratyphoid fever. Having recovered, he was sent to France late in 1916, and commanded J Battery of the Royal Horse Artillery until the end of the war. He was awarded the MC and Bar.

There was no military tradition in the Willett family (the family name was Catt until it was changed in 1863), but plenty of military and naval tradition in Nita's ancestry. Her mother's maiden name was Hoste, and her grandfather, Major General Dixon Hoste, served in the Crimean War of 1854–55 and was present at the battles of the Alma, Balaclava and Inkerman and the siege of Sevastopol; he was a son of Sir George Hoste, who arrived at Waterloo at 4.00 on the morning of the battle and was appointed Commanding Royal Engineer to the Prince of Orange, the commander of I Corps. After the battle he was Mentioned in Despatches and made a Companion of the Order of the Bath on the recommendation of the Duke of Wellington.

The staunchly Protestant Hoste family arrived in England late in the sixteenth century when they fled from Bruges in the Low Countries to escape the persecution of the fanatically Catholic Spanish Governor, the Duke of Alva. They became prominent members of the Norfolk county gentry, and owned Sandringham, now a royal residence, for a century and a half before selling it in 1834.

No member of the Hoste family gained distinction in the armed services until the end of the eighteenth century when William Hoste joined the navy. William was patronized by their Norfolk neighbour Horatio Nelson, and the pair became a kind of mutual admiration society. William Hoste was a midshipman on Nelson's ship *Captain* at the battle of Cape St Vincent in February 1797, when a brilliantly opportunistic manoeuvre by Nelson facilitated a British victory over a numerically superior Spanish fleet, and was a lieutenant on the *Theseus* when a British fleet under Nelson destroyed the French fleet at Aboukir Bay in August the following year. After that battle he was given his first command, the brig *Mutine*, when he was only eighteen years old.

William missed the decisive battle of Trafalgar as he was on a diplomatic mission to the Dey of Algiers, and was greatly distressed when he heard of the death of his friend and sponsor Nelson in that battle. Six years later he achieved notable victory of his own when his squadron of four frigates defeated a larger French squadron off the island of Lissa in the Adriatic, capturing two frigates and destroying another. When the two opposing squadrons were approaching each other head-on in the early morning light of 13 March 1811, Hoste, in a striking evocation of his late mentor, had this signal raised to the masthead of his ship *Amphion*: 'Remember Nelson'. He continued his naval career until his death in 1828, having being created a baronet. His two brothers, the engineer colonel George and Thomas, a captain in the navy, also had successful careers in the services.

William Hoste's life was first recorded in the biography *Service Afloat* written by his wife Lady Harriet Hoste, a descendant of the eighteenth-century Prime Minister Walpole. His naval exploits were noteworthy in an age of great sea captains, though he did not quite measure up to the most outstanding of them. Sir William Napier, the historian of the Peninsular War, wrote of him a little disparagingly: 'He was unquestionably a very able seaman, a very bold man … still he is not a great man.' Tom Pocock summed up his qualities in his biography *Remember Nelson*: 'William Hoste was mourned by those who had known him as a generous and charming friend, a bold commander and a man of deep loyalties.' Not a great man, perhaps – but near enough to greatness, to bring much honour to his family.

Chapter Two

In the Ranks

My army career began on a note of farce. Papers delivered at my home in Somerset summoned me to report at a certain time on a certain day in August 1940 at a barracks in Maidstone, in the north of Kent. That was a mistake. I should have been directed to report at Shorncliffe, adjacent to Folkestone on the south coast of Kent. So the next morning I was put on a train, together with a dozen other misdirected recruits. The train meandered across the Garden of England through hopfields and orchards, with agonizing slowness. It was as if time and destination did not matter. The words of a song of the Mills Brothers, the black American jazz and folk vocal quartet, kept running through my head:

> Put on your old grey bonnet
> With the blue ribbon on it
> And we'll hitch old dobbin in the shade.
> Through the fields of clover
> We'll go down to Dover
> On our golden wedding day.

Except, of course, that it was not Dover but Shorncliffe, a few miles down the coast that we were making for. A more succinct comment in soldier's vernacular came from one of the other recruits: 'It's like Fred Karno's fucking army.'

Fred Karno was an impresario whose discoveries included such stars of comedy as Charlie Chaplin and Laurel and Hardy, and Fred Karno's army was a humorous nickname given to the new army raised in the First

World War and martyred on the Somme in 1916. It became a byword for anything chaotic or disorganized, and I was to hear it invoked repeatedly during the five months I spent in the ranks of the 4th and 6th Cavalry Training Regiments.

On arrival at Shorncliffe in the afternoon we were met at the station by a sergeant and shepherded into the ancient cavalry barracks where the 4th Cavalry Training Regiment was stationed. Immediately I was overcome by a feeling of utter desolation. No officer was to be seen, and the NCOs who took charge of us, taking us to the quartermaster's stores to be fitted with uniforms, bedding and other routine matters, were cold, impersonal and brutal in manner. In place of the side hats and battle-dress that were regulation in the rest of the army, we were dressed in peaked caps and tunics with brass buttons, needing daily polishing, down the front. For the first time in my life I felt totally alone and friendless, with no womb to crawl into for comfort and reassurance.

I need to explain how, in the era of mechanical warfare, I came to be in a horsed regiment. In the early part of the Second World War most countries retained a cavalry element, and Britain was no exception. At the outbreak of war, when I was still up at Cambridge, I was accepted for a future commission in my local regiment, the North Somerset Yeomanry, which went out to Palestine with the 1st Cavalry Division in the autumn of 1939. By the time I came down from the university in June 1940 it had been decreed that anyone aspiring to a commission in a horsed regiment must first serve four months in the ranks, which accounted for my posting to the 4th Cavalry Training Regiment at Shorncliffe; but soon after I had been called up a further decree put an end to all further commissions in horsed regiments. In a military game of snakes and ladders I had landed firmly on a snake and was stranded with no clear prospects of ever getting a commission in any arm of the services.

So Shorncliffe for me was a dead-end. Its extensive cavalry training grounds resembled an Indian *maidan* on which instruction in equitation, cavalry manoeuvre and sword drill proceeded, while far overhead the rival air fleets had begun to clash in the Battle of Britain. The contrast between cavalry drills, practically unchanged for centuries, and aerial combat of unprecedented ferocity in the sky above was extreme. At times we could pick out the minute specks of German bombers, glinting in the sunlight of that brilliant summer, as they flew relentlessly to raid fighter airfields or East End docklands; and occasionally we could see fighters break into one of the enemy formations and a bomber spin out of control with plumes of black smoke spreading behind it as it plunged earthwards like a falling leaf.

A thick thorn hedge separated one part of the *maidan* from a fighter field where Hurricanes were parked along the hedge like rabbits outside a warren. When they were scrambled for action there was frantic activity beyond the hedge. In no time they set off with a roar, bouncing over the rough infield more like robins than rabbits until they turned at the field's end and accelerated one by one down the grass runway with the engines soon rising to a crescendo of sound, to take off and soar upwards into the azure summer sky, soon to be lost to our view.

If the Germans had won the Battle of Britain and Operation SEA LION, the planned invasion of Britain, had followed, the 4th Cavalry Training Regiment could have shown no more than token resistance. Each man was equipped with a rifle but only ten rounds of ammunition per man were available. In fact there was no evidence of resistance being contemplated. No trenches were dug, no strong points organized, no reconnaissance done, no preparation or plans made, at least as far as the rank and file were informed. It was all extraordinarily irresponsible and more amateurish than Dad's Army.

Shorncliffe Barracks were built in the days of solid military architecture. Accommodation was in mellow red-brick two-storey blocks. I was allocated to a second-floor barrack room. It had a bare wood floor and a dozen iron bed frames down either side. Nearly all the troops were wartime conscripts and I was the only wartime volunteer. There was also one old-time regular, Pearson, the room orderly, whose job it was to keep the barrack room clean and tidy. Pearson was a taciturn fellow who suffered from chronic boils on his neck, probably resulting from ineradicable toxins in the blood endemic in some insalubrious tropical station.

In such an all-male society there were bound to be homosexual tendencies. Two middle-aged sergeants flirted shamelessly with Trumpeter Gall, a ruddy faced eighteen-year old, round the pool table in the canteen. If, when and where their affairs were consummated I was unable to discover. Heterosexual love fitted the mindset of most of the other ranks better, as this piece of dialogue demonstrated. Trooper A, as we may call him, was on his way down to the cookhouse for his tea meal, and met Trooper B, on his way back from the cookhouse having had his tea meal, the last meal of the day.

Trooper A: 'What's for tea mate?'
Trooper B: 'Fish.'
Trooper A: 'Fucking hell! Fucking fish! I'm meeting my tart tonight, and you can't shag on fucking fish.'

Trooper A was lucky to have a tart, which meant a regular girlfriend, not a prostitute. The vast majority had no tart and, as far as I know, no professionals were available in Folkestone.

Each day began with reveille played by Trumpeter Gall. Immediately the troop sergeant, who must have been already dressed in his private room, appeared in the doorway shouting, 'Wakey, wakey. Rise and shine,' and if the response was not instant, 'What's the matter with you? Rise and shine.' There was a rush to dress and make beds, and five minutes later we fell in outside the barracks to be marched down for morning stables.

Only Pearson was unaffected by the reveille call. While the rest of us hustled and bustled, Pearson remained inert in bed, invisible under his blankets except for the crown of his head, and ignored by the sergeant. It seemed that he was there for a long lie-in. But when we returned from the tasks an hour later he had shaved, and breakfasted, had swept the room and cleaned the lavatory, and was reading the football page of a week old newspaper.

I paid Pearson half-a-crown a week to clean my kit which he did with an old soldier's efficiency so that I was the best turned-out trooper in the block. Smithson, the occupant of the bed next to me was the most disgruntled man. Small, thickset and black-haired, Smithson complained about everything all the time – the food, the routine, the horses. He had never had anything to do with horses in his life before he was conscripted, so why he was posted to a cavalry unit was a Karno-like mystery. 'We're just fucking donkey wallopers,' he would moan.

One afternoon after the dinner meal when we had time off to rest in the barrack room, a big air battle raged overhead. A formation of German bombers had been intercepted as it crossed the coast and Spitfires, evading the Messerschmitt escort, got in amongst them with deadly effect. The noise was deafening, the sky dotted with falling planes, plumes of black smoke and flames. Smithson, standing on his bed to get a clear view through the window, was beside himself with excitement. 'Look at that bugger. That bugger's had it. Fucking hell! There's another fucker copped it. Fucking awful, ain't it?' Pearson was bent low over my pair of boots that he was cleaning, carefully massaging polish into the toecaps. 'It's fucking awful language, certainly,' he remarked without looking up.

Ackroyd was an East-ender and his mother, younger brother and sister were living in the Docklands. When the daylight raids began he became more and more silent and preoccupied. One morning he left the barracks without a word to anyone and was never seen again. After a week he was posted as a deserter in regimental orders.

Miller was an ebullient Mancunian, devoted to his native city and a severe critic of southern England, particularly its cafes and eating houses. 'Oop in Manchester you get a damn good meal for fuck all. Down 'ere you get fuck all when you've paid for it,' he observed. His true love was dancing, but he had no opportunity to dance at Shorncliffe.

Corporal Yarnold was our riding instructor and a man for whom I developed a great respect. He was erect with regular handsome features, immaculate in his turn-out, a natural polished horseman and an articulate, compelling instructor. He effortlessly mastered the names of all the new recruits in the squad and gave crisp decisive directions. He seemed to me vastly superior as a soldier and an individual to all the sergeants that we came in contact with.

One night I was on guard duty at the main gate. There was a full moon and, standing just inside the gate, I could see well down the road towards Folkestone. There was a profound silence; presently though, I became aware of voices approaching on the road from the town. There was laughter, snatches of bawdy song, cursing and the sound of blows. The noise got louder and louder until three figures, two sergeants supporting a sagging figure between them, came to a halt outside the gate. Roused by the commotion, the sergeant on guard duty emerged from the guard room and went to the gate. 'Let us in, mate,' said one of the sergeants in a drunken drawl. The guard sergeant slipped back the bolt and opened the gate for the sergeants to enter with their sagging burden. As they began to walk towards the barrack building the central, supported, figure gave a huge belch, and then was copiously sick down the front of his uniform and his boots. Moments later he tried to break into song again. 'Stuff it, Yarny,' one of the sergeants told him. The threesome slowly disappeared from view, the guard sergeant returned to the guard room, and silence resumed. A week later regimental orders included a notice that Corporal Yarnold had reverted to the rank of trooper at his own request. He was no longer our riding instructor and his place was taken by a sergeant with a fierce bark and little professional skill.

There were officers in the regiment but they were seldom seen and had no contact with the rank and file. A few were aristocratic layabouts, like the Duke of Marlborough and the Earl of Carnarvon, who resembled a fat frog. From time to time Carnarvon put in an appearance on the *maidan*, tapping his highly polished riding boots with a light cane and strutting around with an air of importance. Our time at Shorncliffe came to an end in late September when the whole regiment was involved in a move. Perhaps the authorities had recognized the inadequacy of a virtually unarmed cavalry training regiment as an anti-invasion force. The horses went first, entrained in cattle trucks and attended by a skeleton squad of regular NCO grooms. It was the turn of the human element the next morning. In accordance with military practice we were marched, packs slung from our shoulders, to the railway halt adjoining the barrack area and entrained with plenty of time to spare. We sat there, eight to a compartment, idle and uninformed, for what seemed an age. Pearson sat opposite me, his neck tightly bandaged, bolt upright like a grand old Victorian lady in her choker. At last there were signs of an officer with a mission: the OC Train. He was a squat, middle-aged captain who paced impatiently up and down the platform. An orderly was visible sitting at a telephone inside the station office. From time to time he emerged and spoke urgently to the OC Train, presumably delivering a message from some distant and Olympian headquarters. In between times the OC Train vigorously picked his nose, examining the pickings on his forefinger with the intentness of a prospector with a specimen of ore.

At last there was activity. The engine hooted, the guard waved a green flag, the OC Train entered his first-class compartment, and the train began to move slowly from the station. We passed the backs of semi-detached houses, out into a countryside of apple orchards. After a mile or so the train slowed to a walking pace and then came to a dead stop. The engine emitted a cloud of steam with a sound like an expiring sigh. I stood up, went to the window, loosened the leather strap and lowered it. For moments there was absolute silence broken only by the thud of a late apple falling from a nearby tree. Then the piercing sound of Folkestone's air-raid sirens became audible, followed by the remorseless drone of scores of bomber engines and the crack of anti-aircraft fire.

Presently the train began to move again, and this time it did not stop, winding its way on secondary lines through southern and central England. At Birmingham (Snow Hill) we were sustained with tea and sandwiches by uniformed ladies. By the evening we were encamped in Thoresby Park, in the Dukeries twenty miles north of Nottingham. The Dukeries comprised four neighbouring houses and estates in Sherwood

Forest once owned by dukes, and Thoresby was the seat of the Duke of Kingston in the eighteenth century. The present Thoresby Hall was a Victorian House and was converted into a hotel in 2000. The hall was out of sight and out of bounds for the 4th Cavalry Training Regiment in 1940.

Not a drop of rain had fallen in the golden late summer of 1940 which I spent at Shorncliffe, when the Battle of Britain wrote a dramatic page in history and the 4th Cavalry Training Regiment added a token footnote to the hostilities. The weather broke soon after we reached Thoresby Park, and once it had started to rain it did not let up for weeks. The horse lines, in a wooded part of the park, were trampled into a morass and the tents, each accommodating eight men, stood in lakes of water. Pearson had vanished. I never saw him again; perhaps he had been sent to hospital for more radical treatment for his boils. Mortimore, a Devon farmer's boy, had taken on the job of doing my cleaning and polishing for the same fee of half-a-crown. For hours on end he squatted on his blankets in the tent, dampness and raindrops everywhere. There was nowhere to go and nothing to do. Life was pointless and miserable for man and beast. One wet night a horse went down with colic, writhing in agony in a sea of mud, while a corporal strove unsuccessfully by torchlight to get him on his feet. It was a scene of utter dereliction.

The cookhouse was kept reasonably dry in an open-sided marquee, but the queue to be served stretched far outside with gas capes providing only partial shelter from the rain. We shuffled forward through sodden ground that became increasingly muddy. 'Glad you joined?' asked the corporal cook in a sarcastic tone each time I reached the head of the queue and held out my mess tin for a ladleful of stew.

In the early days of the Second World War there was no mass volunteering for the services or formation of Pals' battalions such as there had been in 1914. Attitudes to volunteering had acquired clearly defined class boundaries. In 1939 the members of the upper and middle classes volunteered automatically, and not to volunteer was unthinkable. Among members of the working classes volunteering was not perceived as an option; it was unthinkable. Patriotism and patriotic duty were terms that struck no chord in their consciousness. They had no thought or enthusiasm for opposing the cruelties and criminal excesses of the Nazi regime or its tyrannical rule of continental Europe. 'Holocaust? It was only Jew boys they were killing, wasn't it?' they asked. If England were defeated it would merely be a question of losing an English upper-class overlord and gaining a German one. Life would go on much the same. To volunteer was not only foolish; it branded you as a class enemy. The corporal cook was expressing a general class prejudice. After a month of sodden misery we were moved five miles to drier quarters at Welbeck Abbey.

Until the dissolution of the monasteries by Henry VIII, Welbeck had been a monastery of the Premonstratensian Order. From the beginning of the seventeenth century it had been the property of the Cavendish family and, in 1940, was the country residence of the immensely wealthy William Cavendish-Bentinck, 6th Duke of Portland. It was another of the Dukeries. The same duke had owned St Simon, one of the greatest horses of thoroughbred history. Foaled in 1881, St Simon was invincible on the racecourse and, stationed at Welbeck Stud, became champion sire of winners a record nine times. His very experienced trainer Mat Dawson said that he had never known a horse 'so full of electricity'. That could be interpreted as a trying, if not savage temper, but he could be controlled if confronted by an umbrella or a hat held up on the end of a stick. It is not surprising that he was difficult to manage because his box, which was preserved as a kind of shrine, resembled nothing so much as a dark dungeon, in stark contrast to the light and airy stables in which stallions are kept in modern times. The treatment of stallions, and indeed animals in general, has become infinitely more sensitive and humane since St Simon's days. I passed his box practically every day, as it was close to my squadron's office.

St Simon's box and our horse lines were on the opposite side of the Worksop–Mansfield road to Welbeck Abbey. There were, of course, no barrack rooms as such, and we were quartered in the loose-boxes, formerly used to house the duke's carriage and riding horses, ranged round a large courtyard at the side of the house. There were no comforts and absolutely no amenities or diversions. Only one man, the Mancunian dancing enthusiast Miller, was in his element at Welbeck. The Worksop Palais de Danse (in Miller's parlance 'Pally dee Dance') was five miles away, and Miller thought nothing of walking that distance, carrying his dancing shoes in a bag, for a couple of hours spent in his favourite occupation. One evening, to relieve the boredom of hanging about with nothing to do at Welbeck, I accompanied him. The road was dry, but clouds covered the moon and there was barely enough light to see the way ahead. There was not a sound except the ring of our boots on the tarmac and an occasional gentle sough of the branches of trees behind the stone walls that lined the road. No traffic passed us. In such conditions five miles seemed endless. At last we reached the blacked-out streets of Worksop, a door opened, a rectangle of electric light appeared against which the figure of a man was silhouetted and there was the clink of glasses and the hum of talking. We had found the pub. 'I'll stop here for a pint and join you presently,' I told Miller, who gave me instructions how to find the Palais and went on his way.

The Palais was a large drab hall about the size of a tennis court, dark wood-panelled to head height and above that grey painted walls and ceiling. It was a sombre scene. At one end a platform accommodated the five-piece orchestra, and at the other end a flight of stairs led to a gallery with seats overlooking the dance floor. When I arrived and made my way up to the gallery an interval was in progress. On one side of the hall about ten girls in shabby but colourful wartime dresses stood in a silent group and on the other side a like number of young men were standing, chatting among themselves. Only Miller was in uniform. When the band started up again with a lively quickstep the male group broke up and each man walked across the room, gave a little bow to one of the girls and led her onto the floor to dance. The couples swirled round in huge circles, perfectly in time with the music, holding each other at arm's length, revolving as stiffly as tops. I picked out Miller, the most vigorous dancer of all, easily the star of the show, leaning into his turns, while the graceful blonde girl in a red dress who was his partner responded with equal enthusiasm, head tilted and lips lightly parted. Although there were no more than ten couples, their sweeping strides and movements seemed to fill the hall. When the music stopped the dancing couples halted abruptly and separated, the men gave another perfunctory little bow to their partners and they segregated themselves in their groups on either side of the hall. When the music started again the process was renewed, with the same partnerships. But these partnerships had no sexual or social overtones. To the Palais dancing purist like Miller the dance itself was everything, as rowing is to the oarsman, and the partner is simply a necessary adjunct to the dance, as the oar is to the rower.

Sharp at ten the Palais closed, and all the dancers, male and female, made their separate ways home in the dark: no parting kisses, no arm-in-arm walks through the empty streets. The world of the Palais dancer was totally matter of fact and unemotional. It had come on to rain when Miller and I left the Worksop Palais, and it rained all the way back to Welbeck. We were soaked when we arrived an hour and a half later, and I never felt inclined to accompany Miller to the Palais again. But a good drenching did not put him off.

The 4th Cavalry Training Regiment had come to the end of the road, and soon it was announced that the regiment was to be disbanded. There was no call for reinforcements from the 1st Cavalry Division in Palestine, and indeed that formation itself was to be mechanized in the coming months. But my days as a horsed cavalryman were not quite over. I was transferred to the 6th Cavalry Training Regiment which still had time to run, at Colinton on the outskirts of Edinburgh.

Chapter Three

The Road to a Commission

Colinton Barracks, standing at the foot of the Pentland Hills, is a cavalry barracks of long standing, like Shorncliffe. Like Shorncliffe it had solid brick two-storey blocks to accommodate personnel and long stable blocks, with twenty horses each side, separated by bales (hanging steel rods) on a central aisle. We were summoned to tend the horses at first light and evening by the stable call blown by some Scottish counterpart of Trumpeter Gall. The troopers liked to sing a little ditty to the tune of the call:

> Get down to the stable
> As soon as you're able
> And water the horses
> And give them some corn.
> Don't give them too much
> Or you'll give them the horn.

Though the chances of those decrepit old geldings getting the horn were zero.

At Shorncliffe and the two locations in the Dukeries I had been bumping along on the tail of the snake in the military snakes and ladders game, but at Colinton I at last got my foot on the lowest rung of the ladder. I was a member of a squad of nine or ten given the name 'the potential officers squad'. We were part of one of the ordinary squadrons for riding and stable duties, but otherwise we were segregated under the command of Sergeant Baldwin for training and drill. The squad was under the overall supervision of Lord Butler, an elderly major whose evident goodwill was almost paternal. He was clearly willing us to become commissioned officers, and frequently hovered around while we were on parade without actually adding anything to our progress. One of the potential officers, Renwick, had a huge round head like the stone ball on top of a pillar at the park entrance of a stately mansion, on which some mischievous urchin had daubed eyes, nose and mouth in black paint. His head was so big that no cavalry peaked cap could be found to fit it and he was issued with a side-hat instead. So equipped he did the rest of us a good turn. Baldwin could not memorize our names, but he could identify Renwick. 'Smarten up there, the man in the side-hat,' he would shout, while the rest of us were exempt from criticism.

After some days Baldwin learnt the name of Nigel Knight-Bruce, probably because a double-barrelled name was easy to memorize. Nigel, the scion of a West Country hunting family, was a neat horseman but otherwise somewhat weedy and anaemic looking. 'Wake up, Knight-Bruce,' Baldwin would shout when Nigel turned left instead of right or committed some other military faux pas, 'You're like a wet dream walking.'

My friends in the squad were William Below, a member of the Harvey's Sherry family in Bristol, and Clayton Flint, the son of a Fenland farmer who had made profits throughout the farming depression of the Thirties by the cultivation of three crops: wheat, potatoes and strawberries. William had managed to bring his sports Riley to Colinton, by the expedient of giving occasional lifts to the Transport Sergeant, who in return kept him supplied with petrol in those days of strict petrol rationing. Twice a week after evening stables, William, Clayton and I would get into the Riley and drive down to the centre of the city, park the car, make for one of the railway hotels at either end of Princes Street, go to the bar and order a whisky sour. We must have reeked of horse piss but none of the other customers, mostly officers in uniform, ever raised any objection. After a second cocktail we would go for dinner to one of the excellent restaurants that abounded in Edinburgh. While England suffered stringent rationing, food in Edinburgh was good and plentiful. Having a little bit of private money made all the difference for us. On other evenings out from Colinton I went to the theatre. The revue *New Faces* had been the first show to be put on in London when theatres began to re-open in defiance of the blitz. After a London run it went on tour and was put on in Edinburgh. The 'new faces' in the cast included stars of the future like Judy Campbell, Bill Frazer and Charles Hawtrey, and its songs included 'A Nightingale Sang in Berkeley Square', the most memorable romantic number of the war. The show was a perfect antidote to the rigours and squalor of barrack life.

One day we were taken out on a blanket ride in the foothills of the Pentlands. On a blanket ride there were no saddles, simply a folded blanket secured on the horse's back by a leather surcingle. There were about twenty of us in single file bumping along uncomfortably at a steady trot. When we were at the furthest point, about three miles from the barracks, I felt my blanket begin to slip – at first inch by inch, and then in a rush, ending beneath the horse's belly with me, forlorn but uninjured, deposited on the soft Pentlands turf. I lost my grip on the reins and the horse, bucking, kicking and farting, galloped off out of reach. I was left with a long walk back to barracks. A few flakes of snow had begun to fall and, as I walked, snow fell more heavily and eventually turned into a blizzard. By the time I was back in barracks I was a snowman and soaked to the skin.

That night the temperature plunged and remained below freezing, night and day, for weeks. The snow lay six inches deep, frozen and rutted, round all the open spaces in the barracks. Pushing barrows laden with straw soaked with horse piss and droppings to the dump a hundred yards away was a nightmare. Repeatedly, my feet slipped on the ice and I dived forward headfirst into the stinking contents of the barrow. It was impossible to get the horses out, and their corn ration was severely cut.

Just when the futility of it all seemed overwhelming a break came in my fortunes. One morning we were informed that a senior officer had arrived at Colinton with a mission to interview potential officers and make recommendations. When my turn came I was marched into a small room, lit by a single narrow window, with depressing dark green walls and bare except for a wooden table behind which a tiny brigadier was seated. I saluted, and he beckoned me to sit down on the chair facing the table.

'How do you think we are going to win the war?' was the brigadier's first question. At the time, with the German army dominant in Europe, the British army devoid of modern weapons after Dunkirk and long before the German attack on Russia and the entry of the United States into the war brought relief for Britain, it was difficult to visualize victory, ever. But I realized that a negative reply would not be what he was looking for, so I hazarded, 'Invade the continent, sir.' 'Yes,' he rejoined in an impatient tone, 'but what next?' This seemed to me a leap from the improbable to the impossible, but again I appreciated that that would not be an acceptable answer. So I said, 'March on Berlin, sir.'

The tiny brigadier's face went purple with rage and his moustache bristled. He leapt to his feet, sending his chair flying, raised his right arm, and brought his fist crashing down on the table. 'No,' he shouted at the top of his voice. 'Defeat the German armies in the field.'

After that I was dismissed. I left the room in despair, convinced that I had blown my chances of ever getting a commission. However, the tiny brigadier must have gained a more favourable impression of me than seemed likely from the progress of the interview. Three weeks later papers came through directing me to report at the Royal Armoured Corps Officer Cadet Training Unit (OCTU) at Sandhurst. As for William and Clayton, I never saw or heard of either of them again. War brings people together in conditions of great intimacy for short periods and then, regardless of whether they become casualties in action, flings them far apart again.

Sandhurst, where in peacetime cadets were trained for commissions in the regular army, in 1941 was unique among OCTUs turning out officers for different arms of the service. To begin with, it had a long and honourable history of officer training. When it was founded in 1812 it was in the middle of open countryside with only the small village from which it took its name in the vicinity. It was thirty-four miles west of

London, which was judged to be far enough for the pleasures of the capital not to be a distraction for the cadets. By 1941 Sandhurst, with the adjoining College Town, had grown into a substantial residential town to the north-west of the military college, and there was continuous urban development for five miles from Camberley to Aldershot to the south. But the college still stood in isolation in its vast grounds which embraced woods, lakes, playing fields and heathland covering hundreds of acres. The original building, known as the Old Building, was in neo-classical style with a portico supported by fluted Doric columns, but it had been supplemented by the New Building, opened in 1912 as the need for officers increased with the inevitable approach of the First World War. Other buildings included the Royal Memorial Chapel and a library. On my arrival I was allotted a room in the Old Building.

In addition to the matter of history, Sandhurst was unique in providing civilized amenities radically different from other OCTUs and, *a fortiori*, from the ranks of cavalry training regiments. The retired regular soldiers who were part of the college establishment were still employed to clean kit and rooms; the playing fields, on which we played football and hockey, were kept in perfect order; the library was well stocked, and, most importantly from my point of view, I was in the troop of thirty under Major Tug Wilson.

Wilson was a man of exceptional talents. He had a thorough understanding of how the army worked, a gift for imparting knowledge and a most sympathetic attitude to the cadets in his charge. A Royal Tank Regiment officer in his late forties, he seemed eligible for considerably higher rank than the majority he actually held. He was rumoured to have fallen foul of authority at some stage of his career in an incident involving another officer's wife. That had stifled promotion, but shunted him into the instructor's job for which he was ideally suited. We spent many hours in the classroom with him, where he uttered frequent words of wisdom unassociated with the military syllabus. He liked to stand in front of the huge sash windows, swinging and catching the wooden acorn at the end of the blind cord, and after a lengthy pause uttering some admonition like 'For heaven's sake don't do anything stupid while you are here, gentlemen. They can send you back to your unit at the drop of a hat. But once you have got your commission they will find it very difficult ever to take it away from you again.'

We studied such subjects as military law and man management. We were not confined to the classroom. There were drill periods under RSM Brittain and expeditions under Tug Wilson for TEWTs (Tactical Exercises Without Troops) and map-reading exercises for which we were mounted in 15-cwt trucks and ranged the surrounding countryside. With Wilson in charge they were relaxed and enjoyable interludes, usually including a stop for a pint at some well-placed pub. One day our stop was Chiddingfold, a delightful Surrey village with a triangular village green, the mellow red-brick St Mary's Church on one side and a row of houses including The Crown opposite. The heavily-beamed Crown dates from the fourteenth century, is one of the oldest inns in England and exudes old world charm. It was a warm, sunny and calm April morning, and we took our pints out onto the green and drank sitting on the grass. Wilson moved around the groups in turn, chatting amicably – life in the wartime army had evident compensations.

That idyllic mood was soon to be shattered. We got back to Sandhurst fifteen minutes late for lunch and were told to hurry to the dining hall. In the rush to obey I was guilty of the most crass of errors. It was while I was eating my helping of stew and potatoes that I realized, with a shock of horror, that I had left my rifle in the back of the truck in which I had been travelling. I broke into a cold sweat. As soon as lunch was finished I ran as fast as I could to the vehicle park, found the transport sergeant and asked whether my rifle had been seen. 'Oh yes,' he said, 'It has been handed in to the RSM.' This was terrible news. RSM Brittain was the most famous man in the army, after a few generals, and the most feared. He was a Coldstream Guardsman and had a typical guardsman's obsession with discipline and military protocol. At six feet three inches, accentuated by his rigidly upright stance, he towered over most of the cadets, but his most important instrument for terrorizing them was his voice, a kind of high-pitched, penetrating screech, in which he uttered his words of command on the parade ground. It was a sound that reduced those addressed to trembling wrecks. His first name was Ronald, but did anyone ever dare to be so familiar as to address him by it? Such was his reputation as the archetypal warrant officer that, when he retired from the army after the war, he was much sought after to play sergeant major parts in plays and films including *Casino Royale*, the classic Bond movie. This was the man whose improbable mercy was my only hope of avoiding disgrace. As I hurried towards his house I was conscious of the fact that, after moving a short way up the ladder, I was treading firmly on the head of a snake again. To lose your personal arms was a grave military offence; and I had been guilty of just the kind of stupidity against which Tug Wilson had warned us. I faced the near certainty of a return to my unit, the soon-to-be defunct 6th Cavalry Training Regiment. At the RSM's house I rang the bell, which was answered by his wife of whose appearance and manner I have no recollection whatever. I asked her whether I could see the RSM on an extremely urgent matter. She did not reply, but retreated down a passage and disappeared through a door at the end. A pause, which seemed interminable but was probably not more than a couple of minutes, followed. Then the door at the end of the passage opened and the RSM approached. Hatless of course, he had taken off his jacket, collar and tie, and below his trousers, held up by smart braces, was a stretch of bare leg and then brown slippers. He was rubbing his eyes, obviously having been disturbed from his post-prandial nap. Timorously I told my story. I expected a tirade and threat of dire consequences for my offence. What I got was a yawn and then an emollient, 'It's leaning against the wall behind the desk in my office. You can go in and take it.' Without another word he turned and left me, I sincerely hope to enjoy sweet dreams. I had caught the great man, terror of generations of cadets, in an unguarded moment. It was a more colossal stroke of luck than I deserved. When I retrieved my rifle I gave the butt a heartfelt kiss. How to account for this uncharacteristic benevolence? That's an impossibility. But one thing is certain; his lunch must have agreed with him.

Some days later I was on a drill parade under the RSM, marching to and fro in front of the stately portico of Sandhurst's Old Building. An instructor called Captain Turner, an acquaintance from the hunting field, appeared at my side and after a few seconds said out of the corner of his mouth, 'Do you want to join The Queen's Bays?' At that time I did not know one cavalry regiment from another, but I had to answer yes or no, and, purely by chance, I gave a muttered yes. Twenty minutes later I found myself in the presence of Tom Draffen, the mild-mannered commanding officer of the Bays, who was seeking to recruit officers for the regiment. The dialogue went as follows:

Draffen, 'Do you hunt?'
Willett, 'Yes, sir.'
Draffen, 'With what pack?'
Willett, 'The Blackmore Vale, sir.'
Draffen, 'Oh, do you know Bill Manger?'
Willett, 'Yes sir, I have known him for ten years.'

Manger was a senior member of the regiment, though seconded to the Transjordan Frontier Force at that time. He was a neighbour in the Blackmore Vale country which overlaps Dorset and Somerset. That was the end of the interview. I was accepted for The Queen's Bays. Many would condemn this method of officer selection as outdated, reprehensible, politically incorrect, anti-social, elitist and unacceptable. In practice it worked well, ensuring that the regiment's officers were like-minded, capable of understanding each other and working together, and made for a cohesive and efficient regiment in action. By no means all the Bays' officers were hunting men, but they all passed a similar acid test.

The rest of my months at Sandhurst passed uneventfully. They included a three-week Driving and Maintenance course from which I retained only two pieces of information. First, if your vehicle's exhaust is emitting black smoke, you are using too much petrol, and if your vehicle's exhaust is emitting white smoke, you are using too much oil. Second, if you are running low on petrol, it is no good saying I will go very fast and get there before it has time to run out; and it is no good saying I will go very slowly because you use very little petrol that way; there is an optimum speed that is most economical in petrol. I had no gift for things mechanical.

When the Sandhurst course was finished I said goodbye, rather sadly, to Tug Wilson, a man for whom I had the deepest respect. He wrote in my report, 'Well educated. He should make a useful and reliable officer.' When I read that I thought, 'Thanks to RSM Brittain.'

Chapter Four

The Road to the Desert

I joined The Queen's Bays (2nd Dragoon Guards) on 14 June 1941. I reported to Regimental Headquarters in Marlborough High Street, where I met the adjutant, John Tatham-Walter. I had been at Wellington with John, a fine boxer and cross-country runner, but he was three years ahead of me and in a different house, so I did not know him. He was the most meticulous of adjutants, endlessly making notes on all kinds of subjects in his tiny neat handwriting. He showed no sign of recognizing me, and directed me to A Squadron at Ogbourne Maizey, a village nestling in the Wiltshire Downs two miles north of Marlborough. The squadron was out on exercise when I arrived, so I settled down in the Officers' Mess to read the papers and await their return. I did not have to wait long. Soon there were sounds of voices and the tramping of feet outside and, one by one, officers began to trickle into the mess. The first was Alex Barclay, the squadron leader, a man in his early forties who had been just old enough to serve in the First World War. His appearance surprised me. Naively, I had supposed that every member of the regiment would be keyed up and accoutred, ready to jump into a tank and oppose a German invasion at a moment's notice. But, far from being in uniform, Alex was dressed in the most casual manner imaginable, wearing a peach-coloured short-sleeved shirt, fawn linen trousers and blue canvas shoes. He looked better prepared for the beach at Deauville, where I learnt later that he had been a regular visitor for polo in the years between the world wars and with Tom Draffen had been a member of the winning team at the inter-regimental polo tournament at Hurlingham in 1931. He greeted me warmly and immediately put me at ease. Other squadron officers drifted in – Jimmy Dance, Peter Glynn, Gordon Anthony and

Peter Gill. Months later Jimmy told me that they had heard that I had an honours degree at Cambridge and feared that I would be a pretentious intellectual; but when they came in I was reading the racing paper, *The Sporting Life*, so they knew I would be alright.

Ogbourne Maizey contained the training stables of Martin Hartigan, but he had a wartime job from which he only returned home at weekends, and the stables had been closed down and the horses dispersed. The A Squadron Officers' Mess was in what was the head lad's house in peacetime. Gordon Richards had been apprenticed to Hartigan in the early 1920s. Richards became the most successful English jockey of all time, riding 4,870 winners and becoming champion jockey a record twenty-six times. He was the first jockey ever to be knighted. One day as a teenage apprentice he was summoned by the head lad at the stables, given a written note and told to take it to the head lad's wife. At the house he rang the bell, the head-lad's wife opened the door, grabbed his shirt front and pulled him inside. That was his initiation in the art and practice of love making.

One of the inhabitants of Ogbourne Maizey was the vet David Sherbrook. David was steeped in the racing world, having won the Cheltenham Gold Cup on his own horse Poet Prince and having a close association with the Lambourn Stables of Fulke Walwyn, one of the leading trainers of jumpers. As a vet David had ample supplies of petrol and was able to attend the Saturday race meetings at Newbury and Salisbury, the two courses at which southern regional wartime racing was held. I took care to make friends with David and made sure of a lift to the races. The best horses trained in the south ran at these meetings. At Newbury, for example, I saw the great Big Game gain a short head victory in the Champagne Stakes. He had brilliant speed, winning the Two Thousand Guineas early the next year and suffering his only defeat in the Derby in which he failed to stay. Seeing Big Game, a magnificent specimen of the thoroughbred with powerful, well-moulded quarters, made an indelible impression on me.

A week later I was sent up to London to buy collars. The regimental uniform prescribed Van Heusen collars and I had got the wrong kind. I had to catch a train from Swindon, and Sergeant Dixon was given the job of taking me to the station in the squadron 15-cwt truck, a fifteen-mile drive from Ogbourne. We started a little late, and Dixon drove as furiously as Jehu. We raced through the almost empty streets of wartime Swindon at breakneck speed, and as I stepped out of the truck outside the station entrance I said to Dixon, 'Thank you, sergeant. Don't get caught for speeding on the way back.' 'I won't sir,' said Dixon with a huge grin, 'but I couldn't let you miss that train.' Dixon was a reservist who in peacetime had been a postman at Hillmorton in Warwickshire. Of medium height with a round freckled face, he was totally honest, straightforward, friendly and permanently cheerful. From the day of that journey to Swindon – he also met me on my return – we were firm friends.

My military duties at Marlborough were limited by the fact that I was a supernumerary officer and did not have command of a troop. As the latest joined subaltern I was saddled with the unenviable task of giving a demonstration of tank jumping for the benefit of the Duke of Gloucester when he visited the regiment in July. The demonstration took place on the Downs just north of the town, where a trench six yards wide had been dug to represent a stream. An earth ramp had been built on the take-off side of the trench. A group of spectators comprising the Duke, Tom Draffen and the squadron leaders stood well back to watch. My demonstration vehicle was an ancient light tank in which I stood with the engine running 200 yards up a slope behind the ramp. When Draffen gave me the order for 'go' on the radio, I called 'advance' to the driver and, as soon as we were in motion, 'speed up'. We careered down the slope with steadily increasing velocity and were travelling at 30mph when we reached the ramp and soared over the imaginary stream, landing with a jolt which seemed to jar every bone in my body. I gave the order to halt and the tank quickly pulled up, rocking to and fro on its suspension.

Draffen then came on the radio to tell me to join the spectator group at the double. He introduced me to the Duke, who was wearing the uniform of a major general. I was expecting a few words of thanks or a comment on the demonstration, but he did not utter a word, and all I got was a limp hand dangled to be shaken.

The concept of a tank jump was of course absurd. In the natural world six-yard-wide streams with firm banks and conveniently placed ramps, let alone 200 yards flat or gently sloping runbacks, seldom, if ever, occur, so my demonstration existed purely in the realms of fantasy.

At the end of July A Squadron moved from Ogbourne Maizey into Marlborough where the town's principal hotel, the Aylesbury Arms, became the officers' mess for the whole regiment. We lived there in considerable comfort, thanks in large part to Doris the barmaid. Doris was short, dumpy, auburn haired, ruddy faced and matronly. She made it her business to look after the junior officers, mending socks, sewing on buttons and playing a mother's part generally. She was pert, jolly and fun.

In August the regiment received the complement of Crusader and American General Stuart (Honey) tanks that we were to take to war in the Middle East. However, little active training could be done with them because of severe restrictions on the use of petrol. The most memorable events before our departure abroad were visits from the Colonel of the Regiment, General Sir Wentworth (Jakes) Harman, and the Colonel-in-Chief of the Regiment, The Queen. Jakes Harman had been a regular instructor for the Blackmore Vale branch of the Pony Club in the thirties, treating each session as a military exercise with long spells of trotting without stirrups. By the summer of 1941 he was an old man with thinking buried in the past. Referring to our imminent service in Egypt he asked in a quavery voice, 'Do you still get the Khedive Allowance?' Obviously the allowance was paid to British troops stationed in Egypt in the days of Khedives, the Turkish viceroys. The Khedivate was abolished in 1914, but Jakes Harman had not taken that fact on board. His son Jackie had a pet phrase which he applied habitually to anyone he considered guilty of an anachronism, 'Ring a bell when you get into the right century.' He could well have applied it to his own father.

The Queen's visit culminated in a luncheon at the Aylesbury Arms for which the drink component was a large jug of Pimms cup prepared by

Doris in the bar. Doris had taken infinite trouble, adding, besides fruit, generous splashes from several different liqueurs on the bar shelves. She intended to dilute the mixture well with two siphons of soda water at the last moment. But when the mess sergeant, Graham, called for it she found to her horror that all she had in the bar was two miniature bottles of soda. So it was a very potent mixture that was delivered to the luncheon table. The Queen had two glasses, and it was noted afterwards that she was distinctly flushed. No doubt she had happy memories of her visit to her regiment.

The Queen's farewell visit to the regiment was on 18 September 1941. A week later we sailed from Gourock on the Clyde in the *Empire Pride*, a 10,000-ton Clyde-built fast cargo ship that had been converted to a troopship while under construction and now making her maiden voyage. A Ministry of War Transport vessel, she was part of a large convoy en route for the Middle East round the Cape of Good Hope, because the Mediterranean was closed to Allied shipping. She was to be our home for nine weeks.

The *Empire Pride* was by no means a large ship and, with The Bays personnel, Brigade Headquarters and several other small detachments on board, little deck space was available for exercise or training. Living quarters were cramped. The cabin that I shared with three other Bays' subalterns contained two pairs of bunks, one bunk on top of another, a wash basin, just enough room for two people to get dressed at a time and very little room to stow our kit. Of my companions, Jimmy Cumming was teaching himself to play the recorder, Ben Hugh was teaching himself to play the clarinet and Michael Halsted was in almost constant prayer. The noise was sometimes deafening. In spite of it, I settled down to read *War and Peace*.

The sea was very rough for the first four days out from the Clyde, and I stayed anchored to my bunk. The fifth day was calmer, and I decided to go up to the lounge for tea. There were several small tables surrounded by chairs, and I sat down with Jerry Horton, the commander of Headquarters Squadron. Jerry was easily the oldest officer in the regiment, had won an MC in the 1914–1918 war, and had a relationship with the junior officers which was not far from paternal. He was also a very good sailor. He kept drawing my attention to other ships in the convoy that he could see through the porthole, 'That's the Polish liner, beautiful ship isn't she? I think that grey ship is French. There, you can see one of the escorting destroyers in the distance.' The porthole was heaving up and down through an angle of 20 degrees; one moment I could see nothing but waves, then a ship would come into view, and a moment later the sky. Trying to follow Gerry's instructions I very soon began to feel queasy and beat a hasty retreat to my bunk. Two days later the sea was a flat calm and stayed that way for the rest of the voyage, except for a short time at the Cape of Good Hope. The convoy took a huge looping course through the North Atlantic before reaching Freetown in Sierra Leone after two weeks.

The heat in Freetown, where we remained for three days, was sweltering and extremely humid. I contracted prickly heat, an unpleasant condition in which the whole body breaks out in an irritating red rash from which relief could only be found by lying in a bath of cold water to which liberal quantities of Dettol had been added. Nobody was allowed ashore, and my discomfort was so acute that I was able to take little interest in the surroundings. Forested slopes rose steeply from the huge bay, with paths and tracks winding uphill among the trees and clusters of wooden huts. There were occasional splashes of colour from brightly clothed black women walking along the shore, often with bundles on their heads or tiny children in their arms. Clamorous small boys dived for coins beside the *Empire Pride*. A clammy blanket of tropical heat and rain enfolded everything. I sank into a mood of deep depression. Freetown scored no points on my scale of esteem.

When we moved back out to sea my rash disappeared within a few hours. We crossed the Equator with the due ceremony and, after another two weeks sailing, reached our next port of call, Cape Town. We came in soon after dawn over a choppy sea, and the fresh morning breeze kept Table Mountain, towering over the city, free of cloud and sharply etched against a bright blue sky. The sight was unique, majestic, and the weather was balmy and springlike.

In Cape Town food, drink and petrol were in peacetime abundance. We stayed there for four days and were allowed ashore each day. A line of cars would stretch back for a mile outside the dock gates and move up in turn to pick up a party from the convoy and take them back to a South African home for the day. The hospitality was spontaneous and generous. I had grown a moustache on the voyage. One day I was being driven back to the docks by an attractive girl and thought I would try my luck with a kiss. She recoiled from my embrace with a grimace of disgust. 'That moustache is horrible,' she exclaimed. I shaved it off the next morning. On another day I hired a car with three colleagues and drove out to the wine-growing centre of Paarl. The experience was disappointing. South African viticulture improved enormously in the second half of the twentieth century, but in 1941 the wines were barely drinkable.

On leaving Cape Town we sailed eastward round the Cape of Good Hope where the South Atlantic meets the Indian Ocean. For forty-eight hours the sea was rough where the two oceans met, but we all had our sea legs by then and no one was sick. Then the sea settled and day after day was sunny, warm and calm. Departure from Cape Town had separated two lovers, an army captain on one ship and a nurse on another. At six o'clock each evening they went to the highest available point on the decks of their respective ships and engaged in vigorous waving and kiss-blowing, to the amusement of all those who came out to watch.

After four days, the convoy spilt up, one half with the 18th (East Anglian) Division turning east to make for Singapore and the other continuing in a northward direction for Aden, the Red Sea and Port Tewfik at the southern end of the Suez Canal. The 18th Division had a tragic destiny, most of it disembarking almost straight into four years of Japanese captivity; one brigade had arrived earlier and fought in the battle for Malaya under command of 11th Indian Division. The magnificent battle-cruiser *Repulse*, which was escorting 18th Division's convoy, and which we had admired on the first four days out from Cape Town, was sunk off the east coast of Malaya by Japanese bombers and torpedo-bombers on 10 December along with HMS *Prince of Wales*.

In the convoy bound for Egypt everything was peaceful and orderly. We played cards every evening. In the officers' lounge there were two schools – a poker school and a bridge school. I played poker and did not take up bridge until much later in life. From one of the bridge tables came frequent outbursts of furious swearing. They came from Brigadier Raymond Briggs, who quickly lost patience and self-control when he had bad cards. We ate well; at lunch and dinner there was always an alternative dish to the main course, Goa curry and rice and good mild curry too. All the crew, from deckhands to stewards to cooks were Goans, small, dark skinned men, eager to please.

Ashore at Port Tewfik in the late afternoon we had a two-mile march in the gathering dark, past numerous one-storey native shops exuding musty smells, to a transit camp where we spent the night. The next morning we boarded a train drawn up on a line adjoining the camp. I stood at the window of the compartment, looking out at a landscape of sand dunes interspersed with tufts of coarse grass. An Arab boy wearing a *tarboosh* and a brown *galabieh* came into sight, leading a donkey through the dunes. When he was opposite me he stopped, turned to face the train, lifted his *galabieh* and waggled his penis up and down. 'Ah,' I said to my companions in the compartment, 'our introduction to the mysterious east.' Presently the train began to move and for most of the day meandered across mainly desert country to deposit us at Amiriya, a camp a few miles west of Alexandria. There we were united with our tanks and lorries, and spent a fortnight preparing them for service in the desert.

While we were at Amiriya I was sent with a message to the 10th Hussars, a regiment which with The Queen's Bays and 9th Lancers made up 2 Armoured Brigade of 1st Armoured Division. While strolling through the officer lines of the Hussars I caught sight of an officer reclining in a deck chair outside his tent, wrapped in a scarlet silk dressing gown embroidered with golden dragons. I thought to myself that there was an officer with no intention of doing much serious and uncomfortable campaigning. He was Simon Elwes, who spent several years as an officer in Cairo after a short period in the desert, painting portraits of many distinguished people including General, later Field Marshal, Sir Henry Maitland Wilson, Field Marshal Smuts, King Farouk and Queen Farida, with whom he was said to have had an affair. Elwes was to become a close friend of Queen Elizabeth the Queen Mother, after recovering from a debilitating stroke.

In the bitterly cold dawn of 12 December the regiment's tanks (thirty Crusaders and seventeen General Stuarts or Honeys) were loaded onto railway flats for the rail journey to Mersa Matruh on the coast, 200 miles west of Alexandria. One tank, having been loaded, was standing on its flat with the engine still running, while two of the crew stood surveying the proceedings in the turret. Brigadier Fisher, commander of 2 Armoured Brigade, was standing on the ground nearby, watching the process. He was dressed for the cold morning in cap, scarf, British Warm overcoat and gloves, but still looked pinched and miserable. It is necessary to shout to make oneself heard by someone a foot away above a running tank engine, but the shout also carries audibly to someone ten yards farther off. Gazing down from the turret, one of the crew members shouted to the other, 'There's the Brigadier, poor old sod. He looks fed up, fucked and far from home.' Thus embarrassingly, if unintentionally, described, Brigadier Fisher moved away to watch the loading from some standpoint farther down the line.

Winter desert winds were surprisingly biting, and summer desert winds were unsurprisingly baking. The brigadier's outfit in December was roughly standard for an armoured corps officer, with the addition of pullover, corduroy or cavalry twill trousers and desert boots (ankle boots with soft leather tops and rubber soles). Desert boots were much more comfortable than army issue boots, though I had one bad experience with them, as will appear later in this narrative. In summer successive layers of clothing were peeled off to leave shirt and trousers, but never the shorts favoured by the infantry and others. One invariable item for officers in cavalry regiments was the peaked cap with the regimental

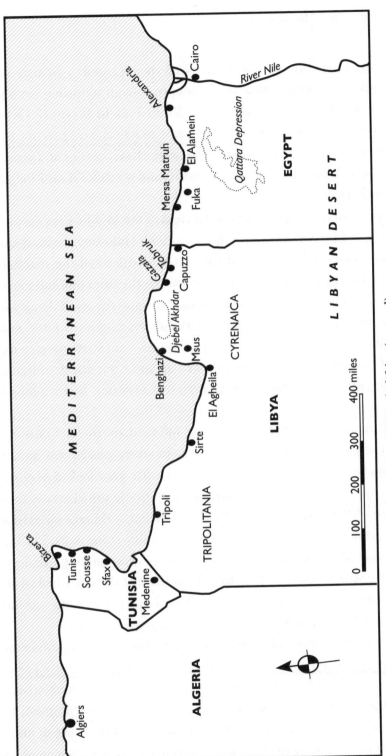

Map 1: North Africa (general).

badge. At times the cap alone identified the wearer as a British officer. The tank headphones fitted over it snugly, though ultimately with some detriment to its shape. Officers in the Royal Tank Regiment (RTR) wore black berets, which were certainly more practical headgear for a tank commander. At Second Alamein there were eleven cavalry and yeomanry (Territorial Army cavalry) tank regiments and seven RTR tank battalions in Eighth Army.

The regiment reached the forward areas of the Middle East war zone in the desert of Cyrenaica early in January 1942. Following the hard-earned British victory in the so-called CRUSADER battles and the relief of the siege of Tobruk in November and December, the front line had moved to El Agheila, a bottleneck between salt marshes and the sea 200 miles south of the principal Cyrenaican port of Benghazi, where the coast road to Tripoli turned through an angle of 90 degrees from south-west to north-west. Our advance to the front involved an approach march of hundreds of miles across the barren desert hump of Cyrenaica. It was a long slow business.

The regiment's tanks led the way, followed by the B Echelon, the regiment's supply vehicles. The going in many places was appalling. One day we crossed a wide area covered with what looked like broken flagstones, then a depression carpeted with dense camel scrub, then an expanse of flat bare tawny desert, then another wide area covered with what resembled the debris of a series of fallen dry-stone walls. The lorries could only cross the rougher areas at walking pace, limping like decrepit dogs. We seldom exceeded 10mph. At the end of the day I looked at the speedometer of the 15-cwt truck in which I had been riding and found, to my amazement, that we had travelled eighty-four miles.

At that time I was still a supernumerary officer without command of a troop of tanks. I was attached to the B Echelon, where my principal function was to lead convoys of supply lorries up to the tanks when needed. The speed of the advance had stretched the lines of communication almost to breaking point. Later in the campaign rations were to improve significantly. We were to get issues of bread and fresh meat several times a week and, sometimes, luxuries like Australian tinned peaches in a rich syrup, but in January, when we were farthest from the supply bases, rations were restricted to the basic necessities: bully beef, hard biscuits, margarine, nasty fatty bacon, excellent marmalade from Palestine, salt, tea, sugar and condensed milk. With only these ingredients to work with, A Squadron mess cook Brooks, who had been a sauce chef at the Savoy Hotel in civilian life, miraculously produced a serviceable Christmas pudding. He was most inventive, and a faithful believer in cooking as an art. He loved to deliver a detailed description of some exotic dish prepared at the Savoy, always ending up with the benediction 'beautiful, sir', like *amen* to a prayer. Out of the line the troops were fed at squadron cookhouses but, in the field, meals were on an individual tank-crew basis. Each tank had a small petrol cooker, and when there was time to do any cooking the standard dish was bully fritters.

After five days of approach march we reached Saunnu and Antelat, two names on the map with no definitive features or buildings. The received wisdom was that we would gather our strength there for an assault on the El Agheila position. The expectation was that the enemy, having retreated 400 miles from Tobruk and Sidi Rezegh, would resume his withdrawal when faced with a determined attack. The reality was very different. Early on the morning of 22 January I was sent with a convoy of supply vehicles to the tanks. There I found that an air of frantic activity prevailed in contrast to the calm that had reigned at halts during the approach march. Tank commanders were busily folding maps, while the crews were securing bedrolls on the flat engine covers of the tanks. I saw Douglas MacCallan, a contemporary of mine at our prep school, Parkfield, who became my best and oldest friend after the war. He liked to present an image of languor and idleness, but in fact was a most intelligent and competent operator and rose to be the head of the coal-mining division of BP. He was stowing kit in the turret of his tank. 'What on earth is going on?' I called up to him. 'A small enemy column has advanced from Agheila,' he replied. 'If it comes on a bit further we're going to give it a bloody nose.'

The truth was that it was not a small column that had poked its nose out to be bloodied. It was a full-scale counter-offensive. The Germans had withdrawn to the Agheila position with only twenty tanks surviving from the Sidi Rezegh battles, but they had been reinforced with twenty-three new tanks delivered through the port of Tripoli while another twenty-two had been unloaded at Benghazi shortly before that port fell to Eighth Army. Then another convoy reached Tripoli with fifty-four tanks as well as crews and fuel. Auchinleck was planning a renewed offensive, which was due to start between 10 and 15 February. However, Rommel was reaping the benefits of a spell of Italo-German naval success in the Mediterranean. Admiral Cunningham's Mediterranean Fleet had lost both the aircraft carrier HMS *Ark Royal* and the battleship *Barham* to U-boat action in November and had suffered the disabling of the battleships *Queen Elizabeth* and *Valiant* in Alexandria harbour in December. The two capital ships in Alexandria had been mined by Italian naval special forces. Since two cruisers, *Galatea* and *Neptune*, the destroyer *Kandahar* and the sloop *Parramatta* had also been sunk by mines or submarines, Cunningham's Force K was temporarily out of action. The Germans had also transferred Luftflotte II from Russia to Sicily and Malta had suffered a period of sustained heavy bombing by both Italian and German forces. The overall result was that the Axis could sail convoys to Tripoli with a much reduced risk of attack by the Royal Navy. This allowed Rommel to prepare for his new offensive which came in late January. His wireless intercept service and Italian and German interception of signals from the United States military attaché in Cairo, Colonel Bonner Fellowes, told Rommel that Eighth Army was awaiting reinforcement and that the armoured formation in Cyrenaica, our 1st Armoured Division, was new to the desert. This presented him with an opportunity to seize the initiative and Rommel was not a man to ignore such an opportunity.

No fewer than ninety German tanks, mostly the admirable Mark IIIs and Mark IVs, took part in the thrust that quickly scattered the light forces immediately opposed to them. They outclassed the Crusaders and

Honeys of 2 Armoured Brigade (The Queen's Bays, 9th Lancers and 10th Hussars) that was the main British tank force in the forward area. The Crusader had a marvellous suspension that enabled it to race across desert terrain at speeds up to 40mph, but was mechanically unreliable and inadequately armed and armoured; the Honey (otherwise General Stuart) never broke down, but was otherwise a pathetic weapon to take on the Panzers. The rival armoured forces clashed on a broad stretch of undulating uplands that resembled grassless downs and featured the insubstantial Antelat and Saunnu and the more substantial 'Well with Windpump'. It was not the Germans who sustained a bloody nose. The 10th Hussars suffered heavy casualties attempting a frontal charge near 'Well with Windpump', and the Bays found themselves, what was left of them, on open ground facing the German vanguard poised above them on the Antelat-Saunnu ridge.

The Bays' defensive position was ill chosen. No doubt there was a reluctance to give ground before being compelled to do so, but then they were fatally exposed. A withdrawal of two or three miles – yielding ground was of no consequence in the desert – to hull-down positions would have compelled the Germans to attack by exposing themselves in the open. In the event there was a twenty-four-hour pause while the Germans regrouped and refuelled. Then, early on the morning of 25 January, German tanks appeared on the crest of the ridge and, in the manner of Byron's Assyrian, came down like a wolf on the fold, spreading chaos and destruction. The hardest blow fell on A Squadron. Peter Glynn's tank was knocked out and Peter killed. The tank of the Squadron Leader, Alex Barclay, was also hit, but he got out unwounded and, after hiding in a patch of camel scrub until the battle had passed, managed to walk with four other unharmed members of the squadron to find refuge with 4th Indian Division at Benghazi. The irresistible German onslaught drove the scattered remnants of the regiment pell-mell northwards for forty miles to Msus, the site of an ancient fort and a desert track crossroads. That inglorious battle came to be known generally as the Msus Stakes.

I was lucky to escape capture during the battle. On the night of 22 January the B Echelon had leaguered – a leaguer was a tight defensive cluster of vehicles formed at night by all units in the desert – on a stretch of downland somewhere in the vicinity of Saunnu. As the last of the light faded we heard the noise of tank vehicles approaching from the north. They halted in a depression a few hundred yards away. Sergeant Dixon and I decided to investigate. There was just enough moonlight for us to keep direction. We walked quietly till we were near the edge of the depression, then crawled until we could see down. All we could discern was the dim outline of vehicles, but we could hear voices distinctly – German voices. We crawled back out of sight and returned quickly to our own leaguer. At first light the next morning we heard engines start up in the depression and then move off eastwards, fortunately missing our leaguer.

Two nights later we had joined the Msus Stakes, moving all night in an endless procession of vehicles, frequently halting, then moving on again for a few hundred yards before coming to another standstill, while green and red Very lights rose into the sky on every side, leaving a message perhaps to someone, somewhere, but meaningless to me. I was riding in the passenger seat of a 3-ton lorry. At one of the halts, longer than most, I and the driver both fell asleep. I woke to see, not the back of the lorry in front, but empty space. We started up and raced ahead, fortunately soon catching up with the tail of the column. In the coming days we made contact with the rest of the regiment and gradually some semblance of order was restored. The German thrust had been too strong for the port of Benghazi, the Djebel Akhdar (Green Mountain) that formed the northern hump of Cyrenaica or the thousands of square miles of desert south of it to be held, and the Eighth Army, of which the 1st Armoured Division and the regiment were part, fell back to a new defensive line running from Gazala Springs on the coast to Bir Hacheim fifty miles to the south. The whole regiment moved back to the Gazala Line, but I was left behind with orders to collect some missing lorries and bring them back to meet the regiment at Rotunda Segnali, close to the line.

Two days later I had collected six lorries and was ready to start on the journey of 150 miles on a due east bearing. I put my faith in a sun compass, the most accurate means of desert navigation, fixed on the 15-cwt truck on which I was travelling. After 150 miles I halted my small column and had a look round. There was no sign of the regiment or of Rotunda Segnali, a conspicuous roundabout built by the Italians, the colonists of Libya, at the junction of two desert tracks: except in the far distance I could pick out through my field glasses a series of black dots that were vehicles. I led my charges there, exactly six miles due south, and found myself at Rotunda Segnali and in the midst of the regiment's tanks. 'You're no good at desert navigation,' I was mocked when I described my movements. At that time we were using captured Italian maps. A few weeks later we were issued with new maps prepared by Middle East Command's own cartographers. They showed that Rotunda Segnali was six miles due south of the position marked by the Italians. My desert navigation was vindicated, but the regiment's success in finding the misplaced Rotunda Segnali was never explained.

Chapter Five

The Gazala Line and El Alamein

'On the night of the 3rd February', so the regimental history recorded, 'the last of our troops were back behind what was to be known as the Gazala Line.' There we remained for nearly four months while extensive minefields were laid, defensive positions dug and improved, and the opposing armies built up their strength like boxers building up muscle in preparation for the next bout. Action was minimal and boredom took over as the chief enemy. A major irritant was desert sores, painful, suppurating sores that broke out mainly on hands and arms and defied treatment. They baffled medical science. 'What ye need,' concluded the middle-aged and ineffectual Scotsman who was our regimental doctor, 'is plenty of fresh vegetables and fruit,' and then added, 'But ye can't have that.'

Several members of the regiment had gone missing in the confusion of the Msus Stakes. When we had been behind the Gazala Line for ten days a truck from another regiment drove into our area, stopped and out of the back climbed Trooper Mitchell, one of the missing men. Mitchell was uncouth, inarticulate, and practically moronic. His writing – officers had to censor the letters of other ranks – was almost illegible, and his wife had written back that she wanted a divorce because, she said, he 'made me do disgusting things'. Yet Mitchell had walked more than 150 miles, without map or compass, getting food and shelter in the tents of the Bedouin encampments which dotted the desert in places where there was water and no fighting, to rejoin the regiment. He was the unlikeliest of heroes.

In spite of Peter Glynn's death I did not take over a troop immediately. Instead I was sent down to RAOC workshops at Wardian, just outside

Alexandria, to collect some specially modified Crusaders. The frequent breakdowns, due principally to water leaks, had given rise to concern in high quarters, and an engineer had been sent out from the Birmingham factory to supervise modifications which it was hoped would cure the problem. His name was Hucker, and for the remaining months that we struggled with those tanks they were nicknamed 'Huckers'. I reported to the workshops' commanding officer, a bushy-moustached major with a hearty manner. 'Nice to see you, old boy,' he greeted me, 'but I'm afraid the tanks are not quite ready for you yet. So could you go away and come back in three days' time, and they should be ready for you then. Frightfully sorry.' After arranging accommodation for the drivers I had brought with me, I made my way to the Cecil Hotel, Alexandria's best and the Mecca for every officer down from the desert. The routine on arrival at the Cecil was invariable – up to one's bedroom, bath, off to the hairdresser's shop for a haircut and shampoo. The shampoo dislodged quantities of sand that might have been expected to block the hotel's drains but happily never did.

After three days I returned to the workshops. 'Good to see you, old boy,' said the major, 'but I'm afraid we're still not quite ready for you. We really do want to get things right. So it would be best if you went away again and came back in four days.' This procedure was repeated once more before at last the tanks were released. Altogether, I had eleven days enjoying a life of leisure in Alexandria, while my only military chore was arranging to draw pay for the men. Alexandria had two exceptional rendezvous, the Union Club where a delectable prawn salad was the lunch-time favourite, and the Union Bar, a superb restaurant for dinner where the speciality was roast wild duck and orange salad followed by fat juicy figs and cream.

The return journey to the regiment in the desert fifteen miles south of the port of Tobruk was uneventful. All four Crusaders covered the 300 miles without breakdown – miraculously or, perhaps it should be said more charitably, thanks to the engineering expertise of Mr Hucker. Hucker accompanied us in case minor repairs were needed: poor

Hucker, he was ill-equipped for desert travel. He was faceless and almost speechless but, to his credit, he never uttered a word of complaint. I never knew his first name, and I have not the faintest recollection of how he looked or how he sounded, or how he travelled back to Alexandria. But he did leave an indelible memory: the Crusader called the Hucker.

For weeks I returned to my job of taking convoys of supply lorries from the echelon up to the tanks, a distance of about twenty miles. Mostly the visibility was clear and finding the way, even in an area devoid of landmarks, was easy. But in March we entered the season of the *khamsin*, the hot south wind that blew from the heart of the Sahara, rendering everything, whether outside or in the shade, burning hot to the touch. Visibility was reduced sometimes to almost zero, by a haze of sand and dust. Once we were hit by a full-blown sandstorm. In the afternoon a huge black cloud appeared on the horizon and steadily approached, growing and gradually filling the sky. For minutes there was uncanny calm, windless and silent. The dust cloud was concave and black, like a gigantic cliff whose apex shone brilliant white in the sun. Then, in a moment, the cloud engulfed us, the wind roared and battered us with stinging grains of sand that insinuated themselves everywhere they could find a piece of bare flesh, and filled eyes and ears. Speech and movement were impossible. All one could do was roll oneself in a blanket, lie low and wait, wait for the storm to pass. And pass, of course, it did, after a time that seemed interminable but in fact was probably not more than twenty minutes. When it had passed there was an eerie silence, the visibility was dazzlingly clear and piles of sand were everywhere – against the wheels and radiators of lorries, against heaps of stones and all over tents flattened by the force of the wind. It needed a full day's work to restore the vehicles to working order and much longer to clean one's body parts in those days when the ration of water was half a gallon per man per day for all purposes. Occasionally the ration was eked out with meagre quantities of water obtained from Tobruk, the deep water inlet and port captured in Wavell's offensive against the Italians in January 1941 and in British hands ever since, though besieged for seven months later that year. Water was plentiful in Tobruk, seeming to ooze rather than flow from the rock face containing the springs. It was far from an unmixed blessing, as it was so brackish that it instantly curdled any condensed milk added to tea and gave whiskey, when that precious commodity was available, a disgusting taste.

At that time the terrain inside the Tobruk perimeter, a fifteen-mile-long semi-circle of wire, trenches and strongpoints whose ends abutted on the sea, was barren desert devoid of vegetation, though there was a small area of cultivation, some olive trees and a few goats when I visited the British military cemetery sixty years later and Tobruk had become a major Libyan port. The Bays' encampment was fifteen miles inland, and every night we were witnesses to spectacular firework displays as wave after wave of Axis raiders bombed the port and British shipping, and ack-ack barrages raked the skies to the accompaniment of constant dull crumps and staccato explosions.

There was a wonderful calm about the early mornings, when the landscape was bathed in a pinkish glow from the rising sun, and every tiniest fold in the ground was sharply etched in light and shadow, and hardly a breath of wind stirred.

One seemingly peaceful morning five of us were having breakfast at a trestle table set up close to the mess lorry, which was lodged safely in a vehicle pit: 'Fruity' Godbold, who had taken command of the Headquarter Squadron from the retired Gerry Horton, Padre Morson, the quartermaster Harry Spencer, 'Tiny' Blair, the RAOC captain attached to the regiment, and myself. We heard the drone of a plane circling above us. 'You want to watch out for this fellah,' said Blair, and a moment later there was a roar as the bomber, a Stuka, began to dive. We dived too, into the mess lorry pit. The bomb fell 300 yards away, close to a cluster of vehicles, exploding in a cloud of black smoke. Immediately there was activity round the vehicles like a disturbed ants' nest. Someone was being lifted and laid out on the sand. I ran across to find out what had happened. Rudi Malcolmson, the quartermaster-sergeant, had been hit. He was lying face down, his head cushioned on his arm, and his trousers had been pulled down to reveal his wounded back. It was as if a sharp knife had pierced one side, just above the buttocks, and drawn straight across his back. There was hardly any blood, and he did not seem to be in any pain. It did not look a serious wound, but three days later he died in hospital. Rudi was a man of great charm, with a reassuring and compassionate nature. Many years later I found his grave in the military cemetery of Tobruk.

On one desert journey the truck in which I was travelling broke down, and Corporal Deakin, of the squadron fitters, was sent out to deal with it. For a long time he bent over the bonnet, tinkering, but the engine refused to respond by breaking into life. In the end Deakin straightened up, scratching his head, a puzzled frown on his face. 'Well,' he said, 'it's got petrol and it's got a spark. What more can an engine desire?' The truck had to be towed in for more thorough examination by the fitters.

Early in May I was appointed to command No. 1 Troop of A Squadron with three Crusader tanks. I was fortunate to have a first-rate crew: driver Ned Lord, the admirably steady son of a pub landlord in Shaw, Lancashire, gunner Eddy Parish, in peacetime a schedule clerk on Hastings and St Leonard's bus company, and wireless operator Corporal Foster, rightly described by his previous troop leader Michael Pollock as 'one of the best'. The squadron leader was Major Lord Knebworth, who had rejoined the regiment recently after a lecture tour in the United States. John Knebworth was a man of extraordinary naiveté, prone to schoolboy expressions and enthusiasms. When told that the day's rations included not bread and fresh meat, to which we had grown accustomed during the static period since the Msus Stakes, but bully beef and biscuits he would exclaim, 'Oh! What a beastly swizz.' By then most of us were desert-wise, and could find our way round as a matter of second nature. For John desert navigation was a mystery, and whenever a troop commander led the squadron successfully to its appointed destination he would express amazement. He was a very irritating man to work for.

As the end of May approached an air of tension increased. Everyone knew that the long period of inaction was nearing its end and it was just a question of which side would be ready to attack first, though it always seemed probable that that would be the Germans. By 24 May the regiment was stationed beneath a low escarpment close to the Trigh Capuzzo, a track which led from the Italian Fort Capuzzo on the Egyptian Frontier eventually to Msus, and a few miles east of Knightsbridge, a cross-tracks marked by a defensive infantry position. The forthcoming battle of the Gazala Line came to be known colloquially as the Battle of Knightsbridge, the focal point around which the manoeuvring armies revolved.

On the morning of the 27th we stood to at first light, ready to move off at a moment's notice. Presently we could hear the sound of heavy firing to the south, and learnt by mid-morning that the entire *Afrikakorps* (15th and 21st Panzer Divisions and 90th Light Division) had rounded Bir Hacheim, at the southern end of the Gazala Line, during the night, surprised and scattered 7th Armoured Division and headed north on the eastern side of our undefended minefields. This was a decisive moment in the desert war. The advance of the *Afrikakorps* to skirt the southern end of the Gazala Line at Bir Hacheim went on throughout the night of 26/27 May, closely shadowed by our armoured cars who sent back regular detailed radio reports on the German progress to 7th Armoured Division headquarters. This should have enabled 4 Armoured Brigade, well armed with two Grant squadrons in each of its three regiments, to take up their prepared hull-down position at 'A', five miles south of Bir Hacheim. But events turned out quite otherwise. Charles Armitage – he became commanding officer of the Bays in 1955 – was in command of a field artillery battery in 7th Armoured Division that morning, and wrote to his father after the battle:

For some incredible reason, 4 Armoured Brigade were not informed of the enemy move, and although we stood to at first light, we stood down at 06.15 and remained dispersed in our bivouac area. Oliver Newton and his company of the KRRC were out at 'A', putting finishing touches to their company position. Oliver crawled out of his blankets at 0600, and looking round the landscape was horrified to see 2,000 yards away to the southwest a seething mass of enemy vehicles headed by an imposing array of tanks bearing down upon him. The enemy did not hang about. As a result a hundred and fifty tanks came sailing over the crest when we were only just aware of their presence. One moment nobody knew the battle was on, and the next moment we were up to our necks in it.

The 8th Hussars were nearest and they had no chance. They were caught at the bottom of a forward slope with no hull-down position and with hardly time to start their engines and face their front. One troop leader was on the ground beside his tank engaged in his morning shave. They fought like tigers but were assailed from three sides, and could not have hoped to compete.

In the event 4 Armoured Brigade was scattered, divisional headquarters was overrun, and the divisional commander Major General Frank Messervy briefly captured. The events of the early morning of 27 May tilted the whole balance of strength on the Gazala Line in favour of the Germans. A few hours earlier the opposing armies had been evenly matched – perhaps the newly-arrived Grants had given the British side a marginal advantage. What amounted to a grave dereliction of duty at 7th Armoured Division headquarters handed the Germans the huge benefit of surprise and had catastrophic consequences for the British cause, resulting in the long retreat to El Alamein and jeopardizing the whole British position in the Middle East.

When at last we were ordered to advance south to meet them, we mounted the escarpment to find, over on our western flank, a large array of enemy vehicles. We swung right-handed to face them. Confronted by the sight of German tanks, German transport and German guns, all with an air of permanent occupation, I was left wondering how it had all happened; how a strip of desert that had been well behind the Gazala Line the previous day had been converted into a corridor thirty miles long and ten miles wide occupied by the Germans in the space of a few hours. And the fact that that corridor was never eliminated despite poorly co-ordinated British counter-attacks, first by armour and later by infantry supported by armour, meant that ultimate victory for the Germans was inevitable. If reports by the armoured cars of the 12th Lancers and the South African armoured cars during the night of enemy movement round the south of Bir Hacheim had not been ignored the outcome might have been different because 7th Armoured Division at the southern end of the line would not have been surprised and scattered.

After a pause in which the enemy were engaged by our artillery, the whole brigade attacked in line abreast. We moved forward at a deliberate steady pace, a dense phalanx of armour which must have been an intimidating sight for the defending German infantry who nevertheless kept up a rapid fire from anti-tank guns and machine guns. The few tanks with the column disappeared, their commanders obviously thinking better of confronting such a vastly superior force. Most of the German fire passed harmlessly overhead, while we sprayed their positions with fire from our machine guns. Soon we were among them, and German soldiers were rising all around us from hastily-dug slit trenches to surrender. We had overrun a battalion of the 110th Lorried Infantry Regiment, taking more than 250 prisoners. It was the only opportunity that occurred in the war for a concerted brigade attack of this kind. This victory in the first engagement of the battle of the Gazala Line was not gained without loss; in A Squadron the tank of Gordon Anthony on the exposed right of the line was knocked out and Gordon so badly wounded that he was out for the rest of the war. During that attack I had felt myself immune from danger, the invulnerable hero of a war epic. That night, contemplating Gordon's wounding, I realized that I was as vulnerable as anyone else and I never felt invulnerable again.

At first light the next morning a cluster of enemy transport, apparently abandoned, was visible on a low ridge to the west, and I was sent in my tank to investigate. They were indeed abandoned, except for one man, who turned out to be a Leutnant Grimm, standing at the back of a truck sorting papers in a brief case. He paid not the slightest attention to my approach. 'Come over here,' I shouted, waving my revolver threateningly. Grimm sorted a few more papers and then turned, and with an insolent air, walked slowly over to my tank. He was a hefty, scowling man, standing well over six feet, probably in his late twenties, and the most arrogant type of Nazi. Looking up at me, he laid his hand on the side of my tank and said in an aggressive, guttural tone, 'You will not win the war.' A moment later Lieutenant Sorbolov, a White Russian serving with the Rifle Brigade, arrived in a carrier, made Grimm get in and drove him to brigade headquarters. When the brigadier appeared at the top of the steps of the command vehicle, Grimm, who had been made to stand just outside, sprang to attention, raised his right arm in a Nazi salute and shouted 'Heil Hitler'. No sooner had the words left his mouth than Sorbolov caught him with a swinging right to the jaw which felled him as if pole-axed. So Lieutenant Grimm passed into captivity, a damaged piece of Nazi goods.

I put high value on my brief encounter with Lieutenant Grimm. Although it lasted no more than ten minutes, he confirmed my received impression of the arrogant, unspeakable Nazi and I could not have obtained a clearer picture if I had spent a day in his company. Was Grimm an exceptional monster, untypical of millions of Germans who blindly and innocently followed Hitler and Himmler to war and genocide? The truth probably is that Grimm was a typical committed Nazi.

Later, during the retreat to Alamein in June 1942, I found myself for a short time in the company of a young sergeant and a handful of men of the Durham Light Infantry who had been captured by the Germans, but escaped. For the sergeant capture had been a kind of epiphany. The Germans, he explained volubly, were essentially decent people. They had given him water to drink from their own scanty supplies; and he implied that he had been conned in the past into thinking ill of Germans when they were really people just like us. I felt a rising tide of anger at his naiveté, but I held my tongue. It would have been a crass mistake to get into an acrimonious argument with an NCO of another regiment. It is true that the Germans on the whole behaved well in the desert, where there were few Jews and no Russian commissars whose presence would incite them to acts of frightfulness. Not unreasonably John Brennan and Colin Smith subtitled their book on the desert war *War Without Hate*, after a quote from Rommel, 'Krieg ohne Hass', and showed a picture of a wounded German soldier giving a wounded British soldier a light for his cigarette. Their commander Erwin Rommel was certainly a chivalrous man. But these considerations could not excuse the crimes of the Nazi regime against humanity or the viciousness of its philosophy. When that has been said, one still has to admire the martial qualities of the Panzerarmee Afrika soldiers, superbly equipped and superbly led. They were simply the best.

The battle proceeded. The regimental history, in a perfunctory note to the chapter describing it, gives a succinct account of our participation:

> The battle of Gazala, which lasted from the 27th May to the 14th June, was utterly confusing to most of those who took part in it and to none more than those armoured regiments. Of these the Bays were continuously in action, without relief, from the opening day until the battle ended. Rushed first in one direction and then another, they never really knew what was happening or even who was winning until the final day.

My own impression was rather more definite, because from an early stage of battle I felt that we were slowly but surely losing. The fall of Bir Hacheim, the bastion at the southern end of the line gallantly defended by its Free French garrison, and of the 150 Brigade box in the main part of the Gazala Line which opened up a channel for the re-supply and reinforcement of the German forces trapped in what was called the 'Cauldron', really made the eventual victory of the Germans, with their superior armour, inevitable. Our long-planned but constantly deferred infantry counter-attack, when at last it was launched, was a disastrous failure.

Although the Bays made many moves in the nineteen days of the battle, probably a week was spent facing the Germans in the eastern side of the

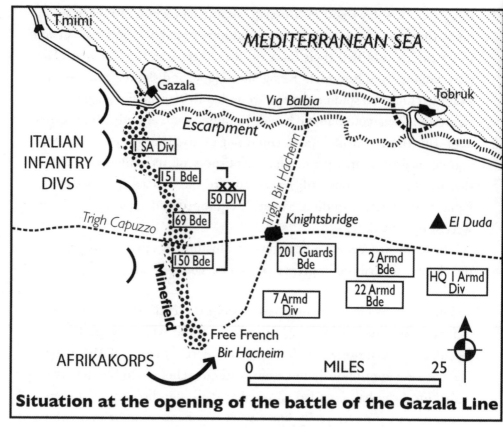

Situation at the opening of the battle of the Gazala Line

Map 2: The Gazala Line.

Cauldron. The days were quiet, but in the late afternoon there would be a furious outbreak of artillery fire nicknamed 'the evening hate', sometimes accompanied by an attempted advance by enemy tanks. One morning, for some inscrutable reason, John Knebworth decided to move his tank – backwards and forwards, to left and right, endlessly, raising clouds of telltale dust when we were supposed to be concealing our position. Finally the Commanding Officer, Tom Draffen, lost patience, and said over the radio, 'For God's sake stop him milling about and get him facing west.'

Throughout the battle Tom Draffen and his adjutant John Tatham-Warter, oblivious to any shot and shell that might be flying about, sat out on two canvas folding chairs fixed to the back of their tank. They were brave men and bore a charmed life, for neither of them was hit during the battle of the Gazala Line. John was very tough, and so were his two siblings. His younger brother, Digby, won the DSO by an extraordinary display of cool courage at Arnhem, and farmed in Kenya after the war. And his sister Kit served in a women's unit in the desert, probably driving generals. She would turn up in her staff car every few weeks. She was cheerful, self-confident and independent. John and Digby were both good-looking in a rugged way, but what passed for good looks in a man seems out of place when transferred to a woman. Kit was no beauty. She was the only member of her sex that we saw for weeks, but there was nothing very feminine about her.

That week imposed a severe limitation on John Knebworth's defecation procedures. The general practice was to unstrap the spade from the back of the tank, walk fifty to a hundred yards, dig a hole in the sand, squat down and defecate into it, cover up the hole and return. That was not good enough for John. He would walk and walk and walk until, to the naked eye, he was a tiny pin man before he achieved the desired degree of privacy. He could not do that at the Cauldron; on one side were the Germans, and on the other three sides various friendly formations.

Compared to the evening hate, the mornings were fairly uneventful. One morning an open Volkswagen was seen approaching from the direction of the Cauldron, with two men seated in it. Obviously they had lost their way and thought they were in German-occupied territory. They approached within 200 yards before they realized their mistake, turned and made off at top speed. Six of our machine guns opened up, the bullets kicking up wisps of sand around the racing vehicle, which jinked right and left repeatedly to upset our aim. It got clean away.

Later in the battle we were on the north side of the Cauldron, occupying a position on a ridge overlooking the battlefield. One limpidly clear morning there was a temporary pause in hostilities, and everything was silent and peaceful. A staff car drove up behind our position, stopped and a man got out. It was Major General Herbert Lumsden, commander of 1st Armoured Division. Slim and neatly moustached, he wore an immaculate tropical uniform with prominent general's insignia of rank, and a red-banded cap. He walked past the tanks, crawled the last few yards until he could see over the crest of the ridge and scanned the distant battlefield through field-glasses for a minute or two. As he came back past the tanks he called out, 'Well, you've got us in a pretty pickle this morning.' In fact we had seen no action that day, but his cheerful demeanour and air of confidence put fresh heart in us.

Later still in the battle we had moved round to the south side of the Cauldron. One evening there was a report of an enemy column approaching from the direction of Bir Hacheim, and I was sent out to investigate. The sun was already down and the light was fading fast. After about a mile I became aware of a column of vehicles crossing diagonally from right to left across my front. I halted to try and identify the column, because the Germans were using many captured lorries, and the presence of British vehicles did not ensure that the formation was friendly. At last I caught sight of a half-tracked vehicle occupied by men wearing Panzerarmee Afrika caps, and I knew that this was the reported German column. 'Switch to send,' I said to Foster, intending to report what I had seen. At that moment there was an earsplitting crash as a solid shot holed the front of my tank, passed straight through the body of Foster, whom I was actually touching at the time, killing him instantaneously and ending up in the radio set. It was a totally silent killing; no sound came from his mouth or his body. He simply doubled up noiselessly and subsided into the well of the tank between the radio and the breach of the 2-pounder gun, an inert shape practically invisible in the dark interior. Life could not be snuffed out more suddenly or more terribly. And, like other Bays' deaths at the time, there was no blood. 'Advance, speed up,' I called to Ned Lord and, as the tank began to move, the next shot carved a segment from the barrel of the tank's main armament, the 2-pounder gun. Foster's body had probably saved the rest of the crew, because it had prevented the shot from either setting the tank on fire or ricocheting round the inside of the tank and killing us all. As the tank started to move, a blue-turbaned Indian soldier, carrying a rifle, rose from a slit trench almost beneath the tracks of the tank, and disappeared in the gloom at a shambling run, a fleeting expression of the terrible isolation of a single infantryman on the battlefield. Far away in some Sikh village a woman, ignorant of Nazi atrocities and the causes of war, might at that moment be thinking of, perhaps praying for, that fleeing Indian soldier. We gathered speed, heading straight for the enemy column, when I found that the intercom had gone dead and I could not communicate with the driver. A collision was unavoidable as the tank rolled on, out of my control, directly towards a German half-track vehicle towing an anti-tank gun. We struck it with a shuddering jolt, the side of the half-track caved in and the tank began to climb over the wreckage. It reached its point of balance, with the disabled gun aiming skyward, and remained poised for a few seconds. I looked down on a scene reminiscent of a Bruegel painting in which human figures are frozen motionless in anticipation of some momentous happening; one man cowered in a far corner of the half-track, while another, directly below me, had one hand braced against the side of the vehicle with the other raised as if to ward off a blow. Then the tank crashed down, crushing everything human or metallic beneath it, before grinding onwards clear of the obstruction. There was no more enemy fire; we must have been shielded from the gun that had killed Foster by the rest of the column. I climbed out of the turret onto the front plate of the tank and banged on the driver's hatch.

Ned Lord opened up, and then I was able to give him directions by hand signals. We drove in a wide left-handed arc round the head of the now stationary column and on to rejoin the regiment with the news that I had been about to give when Foster was killed, but which was now useless because the regiment was under orders to move. There was no time to bury Foster. Night had fallen, but a full moon was up, shedding enough light for tanks in column to keep in touch with each other. After a short time the regiment halted. With difficulty we managed to extract Foster's body from the tank and lay it in the ground where Ned had dug a shallow grave. The corpse's lips were drawn back from his teeth in a snarl like a hunted fox at bay. We were on the Trigh Capuzzo about to bury him and John Knebworth had begun to read the short prescribed burial service when there was a cry 'Come on, we're moving'. We had to lift Foster's body onto the back of the tank, and when it was there one leg slipped off the edge and dangled grotesquely in the half light of the moon for a few seconds before someone succeeded in grasping and pushing it back securely onto the back of the tank. This macabre farce was enacted twice before we were able at last to lay Foster to rest. He was a fine man and a good soldier with all the sterling qualities of a regular.

On the morning of 12 June, the seventeenth day of the battle, the regiment was spread out in a line, facing south, on top of the escarpment a few miles east of the Knightsbridge Box. Opposite us, pressing forward relentlessly towards the fortress and port of Tobruk, was a strong force of panzers while to our left further enemy forces were edging forward in an attempt to encircle us. My squadron, A, was on the left, acting as flank guard. I had taken over a fresh tank with Ned Lord and Eddy Parrish still in my crew, and Trooper Maidment had taken Foster's place as operator. Maidment was well educated and well qualified for the intellectual disciplines of radio operating. He had been Alex Barclay's operator at the Msus Stakes and, though no athlete, had shown determination in walking many miles to avoid capture.

C Squadron, in the centre, bore the brunt of the panzer assault. It was equipped with American Grant tanks, which were infinitely superior to the Honeys they had replaced shortly before the battle. They were equally reliable mechanically, and had thicker armour and a powerful 75mm gun that could take on the panzers on level terms, though its position not in the turret but in a sponson in the hull was a limiting factor. On 12 June, however, they were outnumbered and most of the British armour depended on the fallible Crusader. From my position on the left flank I could watch the battle developing. The panzers, looking like little black beetles against the pale desert floor, crept ever closer, hundred yards by hundred yards, their guns spitting flame and shot at C Squadron's Grants. C Squadron were forced back, little by little, while we on the left had to conform, bending like a pin to counter the growing threat of encirclement. By late afternoon we were all north of the escarpment, compressed into a huddle of the pathetic remnants – six Grants and six Crusaders. The Grants had taken terrible punishment; on Robert Crosbie-Dawson's Grant the marks of nineteen direct hits were counted, none of which had penetrated.

In official accounts 12 June has been marked down as the day the battle was decided, with heavy British tank losses leaving Eighth Army at a hopeless disadvantage. That judgement is misleading. On a purely numerical basis of relative tank strengths it may well have been accurate; but victory for the Axis armies, German and Italian, had really been certain from the fall of Bir Hacheim four days earlier, with Axis strength growing and British strength being whittled away day by day.

That evening brought the end of my participation in the Battle of Gazala, while the rump of the regiment fought on for two more days, to the bitter end. I was despatched to the B Echelon inside the Tobruk perimeter, where first the 9th Australian Division and later the 70th British Division had held out during a siege of seven months in 1941. Crammed with retreating troops and transport towards the end of the Gazala battle, the perimeter provided easy targets for the German dive-bombers, the Stukas. On my second evening there we were having a meal at a trestle table set out beside the mess lorry when we heard the drone of a Stuka directly overhead. As the Stuka began its dive, coming out of the sun, the half dozen of us round the mess table dived too, into a nearby slit trench. The rising note of the diving Stuka was bloodcurdling, culminating in the crescendo of a piercing screech as it flattened out and released its bomb, which landed fifty yards away, enveloping us in black smoke and covering us with clots of earth. We escaped unscathed – with the exception of one man, Michael Pollock, who was partially deaf and missed the beginning of the Stuka's dive and was a fraction of a second late in his dive for the slit trench. A tiny bomb fragment had entered his left temple, rendering him unconscious. As in the case of Rudi Malcolmson there was very little blood, and the injury did not look too serious. However, he died in hospital in Cairo six weeks later during an operation to remove bomb fragments from his brain. Michael's hearing had been deteriorating ever since the Msus Stakes. In April Colonel Draffen had relieved him, to his intense regret, of his command of a troop in A Squadron, and appointed him Assistant Technical Adjutant. With the benefit of hindsight it is possible to see that the appointment was a serious misjudgement and that he should have been sent out of the desert to a post at the base, but he would have resisted that with the utmost vigour. Fair-haired and fresh complexioned, he was quiet, kind, supremely conscientious, sustained by deep religious faith.

The other deeply religious officer in the regiment, Michael Halsted, who had been my cabin mate on the *Empire Pride*, also was a casualty at Gazala, losing an eye and suffering a badly mangled foot when his tank was knocked out in the attack on 110th Lorried Infantry Regiment on the first evening of the battle. Michael survived, and spent more than thirty years in the British Council in many foreign countries. Michael Pollock, Gordon Anthony and Douglas MacCallan were all contemporaries at Charterhouse, so Douglas was the only Old Carthusian member of the regiment to come through the Battle of Gazala unscathed.

I took over Michael Pollock's troop in A Squadron when he was transferred to the technical side. He had a close relationship with Corporal Foster who was killed in my tank at the Gazala Line a few days before Michael was mortally wounded. They shared 'plenty of enjoyments and excitements', Michael recorded in a letter to his brother John who wrote his biography *Fear No Foe*, but 'the most important of all things, his soul, we never discussed'. His missionary urge was as strong as his faith. He wrote in another letter, 'When you are sitting in the desert, with the dust and the wind and the hot sun, the inside knowledge that you are being cared for every minute of the day and night by the Blessed Lord Himself, makes life really worth living.' His essentially simple and straightforward faith set him apart from the agnostics among his brother officers. The large majority of the men were not merely agnostic; they were totally irreligious, regarding religious observance as a class thing, the preserve of toffs. But any officer who did not put on airs, who took an interest in the affairs of his men, who 'mucked in', was accepted and respected. On active service an officer in an armoured regiment shared the same tea brewed on a tank petrol cooker, washed and shaved in the same meagre supply of water in a canvas bucket slung over the breach of the tank gun, as his crew. In the circumstances any officer who did not fit was instantly exposed. Michael's transparent sincerity and goodwill gained him a secure place in the affections of his men.

During the next few days we drove down the Via Balbia, the Italian-built coast road, over the frontier into Egypt. There we were read an order of the day from the Eighth Army commander, the burden of which was that, although we have been defeated on the Gazala Line, all was not lost. The frontier was defended by stronger forces than ever before, and Tobruk was defended by more troops, more guns and more tanks than at any time during the recent siege. Looking out from the truck in which I was travelling, I could see a few soldiers of the 1st South African Division crouching behind what looked like upright flagstones. The rocky ground was too hard to dig trenches. They did not have an air of permanence. The doctrine had been that Tobruk would never be invested again, because keeping it supplied during the siege had been too costly a commitment; but the fortress had become so iconic an object of British prestige that its abandonment was countermanded by none other than Churchill himself late in the day and hasty preparations were made to hold it. During the siege Rommel had concentrated his attacks on the south-west corner where the defences were strongest. In June 1942 he launched his attack in the south-east, where the defences were weaker and overlooked by the high ground of El Duda. He had intended to attack there in November 1941, but was forestalled by the British CRUSADER offensive and the breakout by the Tobruk garrison.

Dive-bombed, heavily shelled and overrun by a swarm of panzers, the perimeter defences caved in practically without a struggle and the panzers raced on towards the harbour. It was all over in a few hours. The defence had depended mainly on the inexperienced 2nd South African Division, commanded by an inexperienced general, Klopper. Thirty-three thousand prisoners and an abundance of stores and petrol fell into German hands. It was a crushing blow for the Allied cause.

Once Tobruk had fallen there was no possibility of holding a fragile line at the frontier, or anywhere in the bare featureless 150-mile stretch of desert between the frontier and the tiny port of Mersa Matruh. Nor was Matruh, isolated on a promontory, defensible though it was protected by extensive minefields. There was one gap in the north-south minefield, for the main coast road, and a major traffic jam formed at it as thousands of retreating vehicles desperate to escape the pursuing panzers, funnelled into it. Everyone patiently awaited their turn – except one man, a Rifle Brigade major in a jeep, who made persistent attempts to jump the queue. 'I am due to be at an order group on the far side of the minefield at 3pm. The Brigadier will be very angry if I am late,' he kept saying to excuse his impatience. 'Stop fussing. We are all in the same boat,' he was told. He was Vic Turner, who earned a VC at the second battle of Alamein in command of 2nd Rifle Brigade that defied the relentless assault of enemy tanks on the *Snipe* position for a whole day.

Mersa Matruh was easily outflanked, and there was a seeming inevitability about the way in which the advancing Germans scattered and by-passed formation after formation that stood in their way in the 120 miles that separated Matruh from the Alamein line. Tankless, I was back on the B Echelon. One day I was summoned by the B Echelon commander, Fruity Godbold, and given orders to take a convoy of six petrol lorries to replenish the regiment, which was practically out of fuel, thirty miles to the west. I plotted my course and set off at the head of the convoy, spread out in single file behind. After going about ten miles I caught sight of the barrel of a gun and a man's head above a tussocky hillock straight ahead. Was it friend or foe? I halted my convoy and went on in my truck to investigate. When I had closed to about 500 yards a shot from the gun whistled overhead. There was my answer, and I rapidly turned about and drove back to rejoin my convoy. Obviously my mission was impossible, and I spent a frustrating half hour trying to contact the regiment on the radio. At last Captain Arthur Rowland on regimental headquarters heard my call, and called back to tell me, to my amazement, that their position was not to the west, but to the east of me. What happened was that Tom Draffen, marooned with the regiment far behind the German front line, decided to drive during the night clean through the German lines, trusting that they had just enough petrol for the forty-mile journey. They drove through or past several enemy leaguers, narrowly missing sleeping soldiers on the ground, and passed miraculously undetected into British-held territory. After I had rejoined the regiment with my convoy I went to report to the commanding officer, leaving my truck 200 yards away and proceeding on foot. I was wearing a new pair of desert boots which had rubbed my heels raw, and I approached the colonel slowly and painfully through ankle deep soft sand. 'What's the matter with your sproggs?' Tom Draffen asked, and from that moment 'Sproggs' became my nickname in the regiment for the rest of the war.

The whole month of July was spent in an inconclusive slogging match on the Alamein line, though this, the first battle of El Alamein, properly counts as a British success because the headlong German advance from Gazala was decisively halted. El Alamein was the most readily defensible line in the Western Desert of Egypt, consisting of a forty-mile stretch anchored at the northern end by the Alamein box on the sea and at the southern end by the Qattara Depression, an area of quicksand virtually impassable to vehicles. The German aggressive drive was nearly exhausted by the time they reached Alamein. Their running tanks were reduced to a handful, and their infantry striving to take the Alamein box were pinned down by concentrated artillery fire. General Auchinleck, the commander of both Eighth Army and Middle East Forces, kept issuing orders of the day, the burden of which was 'Well done Eighth Army. The enemy is exhausted. You only need to hang on and he will be defeated.'

At the time I wondered how he acquired such accurate information about the state of the enemy. He was of course, benefiting from high-level intelligence derived from *Ultra* developed at Bletchley Park but, of course, we did not know about the source until decades later. The German drive was not quite exhausted. One morning when we were in a defensive position just behind the front a straggling column of Indian soldiers trudged past through soft sand, rifles slung over their shoulders, survivors of the overrunning of the Deir el Shein box (a deir was a flat-bottomed depression hollowed out by the vicious desert winds); but the experienced 9th Australian Division had been brought into the line and began penetrating attacks in the north, while at the southern end of the line an attempted push by the Italian Littorio and Ariete armoured divisions was brought to an abrupt halt by the 2nd New Zealand Division.

Gradually the initiative passed from Rommel's Panzerarmee to the British. Auchinleck launched a series of attacks in an effort to achieve a breakthrough. They made some progress, but always ran out of steam and usually any ground gained was lost to German counter-attacks. The matériel to sustain an offensive was simply lacking. During the month-long battle of First Alamein the Bays were never in the field as a coherent unit. Sometimes we could muster a squadron, which would join squadrons of the other two regiments in the brigade to form a composite regiment. Replacement tanks emerged in a regular flow from the Wardian workshops, but they were hastily repaired tanks that had been knocked out or had broken down, and often broke down again even before they had reached the forward units. John Knebworth was killed when in command of a composite squadron from the Bays and the 4th Hussars on the Miteiriya Ridge, immediately south of the Alamein box. He had just taken the surrender of a large group of German infantry when his tank was hit and burst into flames, and he was shot and mortally wounded as he tried to make his way back to safety on foot. These circumstances led to a report that John was shot by enemy troops who had surrendered and were technically prisoners of war, but this does not allow for the fact that his tank was knocked out by an anti-tank gun that was not included in the surrender, and nobody knows where the bullet that killed him came from. With all his limitations, John was a very brave and conscientious officer.

One of the most serious British failings was the absence of any communication between armour and infantry. A significant example of how costly this could be emerged from an account by the New Zealand Brigadier Howard Kippenberger, who later briefly commanded 2nd New Zealand Division in Italy, and, after the war, became Editor-in-Chief of the *Official History of New Zealand in the Second World War*. His brigade had made a night attack on the Ruweisat ridge, a prominent rocky feature stretching for several miles due east from the Alamein line. The attack was successful, and was pushed on to the western end of the ridge, only to be cut off with heavy losses by a German dawn counter-attack. Kippenberger was viewing the later stages of the battle from his command tank when Herbert Lumsden, commanding 1st Armoured Division, drove up in his staff car, mounted Kippenberger's tank and asked for news of the battle. Kippenberger exploded. He said that he had been promised that the tanks would be up with his infantry before first light to protect them against counter-attack, but there had been absolutely no sign of them; it was a disgrace. Lumsden stepped down from the tank and walked towards his staff car, as Kippenberger imagined with the intention of radioing orders for immediate action by the armour. Instead he unstrapped a spade from the back of the car, raised it and brought it down with sickening force on a scorpion crawling across the sand, replaced the spade and drove away.

The fact was that the regiment had received no warning of the New Zealand attack and no orders to support it. Later that day Jackie Harman, then commanding A Squadron, visited regimental headquarters (RHQ), and when he returned told me, 'The New Zealanders did an attack last night, but they pushed on too far and got cut off.'

On 26 July the Bays, then consisting of A Squadron and a squadron of 9th Lancers, was involved in Operation MANHOOD, also known as the Auk's last battle. Auchinleck's plan was for an infantry attack by the Australians, the South Africans and the British 69 Brigade to punch a hole in the Axis defences through which the armour would pass and exploit their success in open country beyond. The plan was an expensive failure – to many minds a predictable one at that. The resources for such an ambitious operation were lacking. Even if the infantry had punched a gap in the mine-fields, which they did not do, the small numbers of decrepit tanks available were far too few for successful exploitation. From the armour's point of view the organization was chaotic. Illuminated lanes were intended to guide the tanks from their assembly areas to the minefield gap, but many of the lights were missing, unlit or had gone out, and finding the way was a very slow business. When day broke we were still far on the starting side of the minefield, and after we had remained stationary waiting for orders for most of the morning, the operation was called off. From our point-of-view, the Auk's last battle was virtually a non-starter. Much criticism was levelled at the performance of the armour. That criticism was based on ignorance of the limitations imposed by clapped-out tanks, the fact that the armoured formations were mostly hastily assembled composite squadrons or regiments, and the lack of co-ordinated effort in the army as a whole.

The Auk's last battle brought to an end the Battle of First Alamein, when stroke and indecisive counterstroke had followed each other for almost the full month of July. The front settled down to a stalemate while the centre of gravity shifted to Cairo and the re-organization of the higher command. Auchinleck got the sack. Tall and square-faced with a clipped moustache, he looked the very picture of a professional officer. He had a commanding presence, and was determined, pragmatic and clear-sighted. His greatest failing was in his choice of subordinates. His appointment of Neil Ritchie, who had never before held command of troops in the field, to command Eighth Army at a critical stage of the CRUSADER battle in November 1941, was a mistake. Ritchie's appointment was premature rather than fundamentally wrong. Later in the war he redeemed his reputation as a corps commander in northern Europe.

Winston Churchill and the Chief of the Imperial General Staff, Alan Brooke, were in Cairo in early August orchestrating the necessary changes. Churchill's first choice for command of Eighth Army, 'Strafer' Gott, was killed when the plane taking him to Cairo to meet Churchill was shot down. It is now known that this was not a chance encounter with a German aircraft but a planned attack on the plane in which the Luftwaffe, through intercepting a message broadcast *en clair*, knew that he would be travelling. Gott was a rifleman, and all loyal members of the Rifle Brigade and the KRRC have argued passionately that he would have fought the battle of Second Alamein differently and more effectively than Monty. The validity of that argument is questionable. Gott had made his reputation when the fighting flowed to and fro over the wide open spaces of the desert. His ability to fight the kind of set-piece battle that was mandatory on the narrow front at Alamein is doubtful. He himself gave the lie to his supporters: 'I've tried everything I know. It's time someone else had a go.' It was the remark of a tired and disillusioned man.

After Gott was killed Bernard Montgomery was hastily summoned from England to command Eighth Army. Montgomery was not everybody's cup of tea. Hermione Lady Ranfurly, whose vastly entertaining book *To War with Whitaker* threw penetrating light on mainly social aspects of the war in the Middle East, spent many months in the household of General Wavell, the former Commander-in-Chief, in Cairo. She wrote in a letter to me years later:

Wavell had to defend Persia, Iraq, Syria, Palestine and Abyssinia as well as Egypt with too few troops and inadequate arms, and also had to help over Greece – with a non-stop barrage of criticism and interference from Churchill. It was Wavell who held this huge fort. Monty was more fortunate, greatly reinforced but only stuck with North Africa. Of course, and rightly, you admire the nasty little man, but I shall always believe that Wavell was the giant in those days and never a nasty little man.

Among the faults she found in Monty was 'deliberately trying to steal everybody else's thunder'.

The points she made were not without validity, but the comparisons she made between the two men were open to challenge because the responsibilities they shouldered were radically different, and called for different gifts and qualities. If their roles had been reversed it is doubtful whether either would have emerged with a shining reputation. Whereas, for Monty, self-advertisement was a necessary part of the mystique of generalship, for Wavell it was anathema. Hermione found Monty insufferably rude and arrogant, and his lack of social graces made him unwelcome in the higher reaches of Cairo society, but ostracism would not have worried him in the least. He was in the Middle East with one aim, and one aim only – to defeat the German Panzerarmee, and specifically its commander, Erwin Rommel, in the field. For that purpose his professionalism, his genius for planning and his ability to inspire his troops, qualified him ideally.

They were both great men, but strongly contrasting personalities. They not only served in the Middle East in different circumstances and commands, they were in the Middle East at different times. Wavell was dismissed as Commander-in-Chief Middle East in July 1941, and Monty did not arrive in the Middle East to take command of Eighth Army until over a year later, when the German Panzerarmee was 250 miles closer to Cairo, the site of Middle East Headquarters. Afterwards Wavell became Viceroy of India, a civilian post of an eminence to which Monty never aspired. Wavell was taciturn, undemonstrative, a lover of poetry and literature who published an anthology of great poems entitled

Other Men's Flowers. It is impossible to visualize Monty, interested in little except war and the making of war, doing anything similar.

I spent practically the whole of August with A Squadron, guarding minefields at the extreme southern end of the Alamein line. To our left stood the bare, white, steep-sided bulk of Qaret El Himeimat, and from Himeimat an equally bare plateau extended westwards. An Italian unit romantically entitled the 'African Hunters' was reported to be active on the plateau, but we never saw any sign of them. The ground on our side of the minefield was broken, with many small wadis, hillocks and sand dunes. We were at pains to conceal our presence from the enemy. The squadron was encamped in a depression half a mile behind the minefield. Each day before first light one troop in rotation would move out to a position close behind the minefield, and the troop leader would then crawl forward to a slit trench on a low ridge overlooking the minefield. There he would remain all day, keeping watch on the flat plain that stretched to the horizon in front of him. There was no shade, and the heat of the midsummer desert sun was scorching. When it was my turn layer after layer of skin peeled off my nose, and by the time we moved back to the squadron at last light I was well roasted. Richard Dimbleby, speaking on the BBC from his Cairo base, said that tanks got so hot in the sun that you could fry an egg on the turret lid. As I never had an egg in the desert I was unable to put this theory to the test.

Early in the battle a number of Italian tanks had been knocked out and remained untouched in no man's land with the corpses of crew members rotting inside them. The place was known as 'Death Valley'. The corpses generated swarms of millions of flies, which transferred their attention to any live human beings for miles around. If you were handed a mug of tea its surface would be instantly covered by flies, and if you spooned them off fresh swarms would cover it before you could raise the mug to your lips. Diarrhoea and vomiting were rife. One afternoon I was struck by severe stomach pains and repeated bouts of vomiting, finally bringing up nothing but green bile. I decided that I would have to report sick the next morning, but when I woke up I found that I was miraculously cured.

The flies were attracted not only by tea and food but by festering desert sores on which they settled thickly, causing intense irritation. Lacking bandages, we tried to cover the sores with handkerchiefs which, after days far from any laundering facilities, were seldom clean.

One day I was sent to the workshops to collect two tanks that had been repaired. On my way back I came to the lip of a *deir* and, looking down at its flat floor, caught sight of a staff car crossing it. An army commander's flag was waving on its radiator, and in the back was seated a small figure, stiffly upright, and wearing a Royal Tank Regiment beret. It was Monty, and in the strangest of ways my spirits were suddenly uplifted and I was filled with a feeling of optimism. I was profoundly affected by Monty's powerful, almost messianic, charisma. Hermione Ranfurly would not have understood that.

The latest-joined subaltern in A Squadron was Derek Cottier. Our orders were to move as little and as slowly as possible on order not to give away our position to the enemy. One morning Derek came swinging into the leaguer in his tank, raising clouds of dust. Jackie Harman, then second-in-command of the squadron, gave him clear hand signals to slow down, but Derek misinterpreted them as a greeting. 'Morning Jackie,' he called out. With his finely chiselled features and slender limbs, Derek was a beautiful officer, but he was also extremely stupid.

As the last days of August approached it became apparent that the stalemate was about to end. Jimmy Dance, in command of A Squadron, was summoned to regimental headquarters and on his return told the assembled troop leaders that Rommel was expected to attack within the next few days. We gave a collective groan. On past form a Rommel attack would bring defeat and humiliation for the British, and we thought that we had fought him to a standstill in July. 'No, no,' Jimmy was quick to assure us, 'this time we are ready for him and will give him a drubbing.' A day later Jimmy went sick and was replaced in command of A Squadron by John Tatham-Warter.

The German offensive began on the night of 31 August/1 September. Peter Gill's troop was in the forward position when Italian engineers appeared and began to lift mines. Peter was perfectly placed for an effective shoot, but when he reported what he had seen on the radio he was ordered not to get involved in a firefight but to withdraw in conformity with the rest of the squadron. The role of the composite regiment of which the squadron was part was not to oppose the enemy advance but to observe, report and lure the enemy on to the main defensive position on the Alam el Halfa ridge farther north. Nevertheless Peter's withdrawal was surely premature and he could have imposed a considerable delay on the opening of the minefield gap through which the two Italian armoured divisions, Ariete and Littorio, were to pass.

The Alam el Halfa ridge lay at right angles to the north-south Alamein line. It had long been recognized as the key to the defence of the line, but in the short time since his arrival Montgomery had strongly reinforced it, installing two brigades of the newly-arrived 44th Division and the tanks of 10th Armoured Division. Halted in front of this formidable position, the German panzer divisions were pounded ceaselessly from the air and by the British artillery, and after three days Rommel had to accept defeat and call off the battle. The composite regiment's phased withdrawal had taken us to a reserve position north of the ridge. When the battle was over we left our tanks at a pre-arranged spot, to be taken over by some other, unspecified formation, and went by lorry to Khatatba, close to the Alexandria to Cairo desert road, to prepare for the decisive battle of the desert war.

Despite its proximity to the greenery of the Nile delta, the camp at Khatatba was a dreary place – a sandy wasteland with a few permanent features like latrines. A native thief caught prowling the camp sought refuge down one of the latrines. His condition when forcibly extracted from his hiding place was sordid beyond description. Two main tasks were our concern at Khatatba. One was to adopt our new tanks; the other was to practise the approach to and passage through minefield lanes which would be our role in the opening phase of the projected battle of Second

Alamein. The new tanks were thirty-two of the 300 Shermans promised by Roosevelt to Churchill to compensate for the losses suffered in the fall of Tobruk. The Sherman was far superior to any tank previously in use by the British – even to that reliable stopgap the Grant: it was mechanically reliable, thick armoured and had a long-barrelled 75mm gun mounted in a turret capable of 360-degree traverse. Two squadrons, B and C, were equipped with Shermans. A Squadron, my squadron, retained Crusaders, more mechanically reliable than in the past, thanks to numerous modifications, but still under-armed and under-armoured in comparison with the improved versions of the German Mark III and Mark IV tanks that were coming on stream. My own tank did not even have a high-velocity gun. Its principal armament was a 3-inch mortar, capable of lobbing a shell 1,500 yards at targets on the ground but useless against armour.

The approach march rehearsals, all night affairs, proceeded to exhaustion – at a squadron, regimental, brigade and divisional level, until we could have followed an illuminated lane to a minefield gap in our sleep. One day at the end of September we were at lunch in the A Squadron mess tent when the squadron leader, John Tatham-Warter, took a sharp look round the table and exclaimed, 'What are you all doing sitting here? Some of you ought to be on leave.' Tatham-Warter was one of those rare professional soldiers who knew instinctively what you could and couldn't get away with in the army. Where most squadron leaders would have applied to the commanding officer, who would have threaded the application through successive layers of command until it ended up on the desk of the divisional general, for authority to send officers on leave when a great battle was imminent, John had no hesitation in making the decision for himself. Accordingly, Jackie Harman, Chris Parker and I found ourselves at 7.40 that evening at Cairo Central Station on the overnight train to Luxor. We had an excellent dinner and afterwards, when the dining car had emptied, a waiter in white galabieh and red sash stood in the doorway and brought us drinks until we decided it was time to retire to our sleepers for the night. It was a glorious contrast to tank life in the desert. We were in Luxor and checked into a comfortable hotel in time for breakfast. For four days we behaved like regular tourists, eating, drinking and sleeping well, visiting antiquities and what in guide's language was 'ze valley of ze kinks' and going for drives in a gharry. Then we had the return train journey by day to rejoin the regiment at dreary Khatatba.

Chapter Six

Second Alamein

The initial phase of the decisive second Battle of Alamein consisted of an attack by four infantry divisions (9th Australian, 51st Highland, 2nd New Zealand and 1st South African) on the strongly defended northern sector of the Panzerarmee's line. The plan was that the infantry breakthrough would be followed by an armoured thrust into the open desert beyond. The Bays, as part of the 1st Armoured Division, were an integral part of that thrust. Things did not work out quite as planned, mainly because the defences, particularly the German minefields, were much deeper than the plan allowed for. Consequently there were twelve days of relentless pounding before the Panzerarmee was finally defeated and wilted away.

My recollections of the battle are fragmentary and are supplemented by a graphic, detailed and hitherto unpublished account of the opening stages written by Mike Tomkin, then a troop leader in B Squadron of the Bays, immediately after the battle. Mike, a highly efficient officer with a lively sense of humour, afterwards became adjutant of the regiment and survived the war. Mike wrote:

The battle began on the night of 23 October. On the 19th we were still a long way back – almost on the edge of the delta. That night we moved up to a place about half way to the front, where we stayed till the night of the 21st. In the afternoon of that day we were all told by the Colonel exactly what was going to happen – including General Montgomery's plan – meaning that ultimately every soldier in the Eighth Army heard what was intended, and what was expected of us all. It was made quite clear that this was a vital battle in the outcome of the war and linked with operations elsewhere. These revealed themselves later with the Anglo/American invasion of North Africa.

On the night of the 21st we moved up to the Assembly Area, which was about 10 miles behind our minefields and near the sea. We arrived at 1am in the morning of 22 October and spent the rest of the day sleeping, bathing and completing our last minute arrangements. Freddie Barnado organized all the maps, of which there seemed to be a vast number, and we got them all fitted into our map cases.

The next day, the 23rd, there was in the morning an address by the Brigadier, who said everything expected of him, and read out General Montgomery's order of the day in which he expressed confidence that if every officer and man entered this battle with the determination to fight and kill and win 'we will hit the enemy for six right out of North Africa'. The operation order came out, and then we had to mark everything down on the maps. Nothing to do now but wait until the evening. We had a very good evening meal, which included a certain amount of Irish whiskey. Everybody very cheerful and in great form. In B Squadron there were the Squadron Leader, Humphrey Weld, George Rich, Douglas MacCallan, Freddie Barnado, David Gay, Bill Yates and myself. We left soon after 7pm. We moved up quite slowly along our route. We were the leading squadron with some scout cars in front of us. At 9.40 the artillery barrage began and, although we were still a good way behind, it was fantastic in its intensity. The whole sky was lit up by the gun flashes. We halted in order to top up with petrol. It was now about 11pm. The infantry were attacking in front of us and our advance depended on whether they got their objectives or not. If all went well we were to start off again at 2am. I got my deck chair out and made myself as comfortable as possible. Vague bits of information came back – one that the Australians, who were directly in front of us, were going very strong and had got all their objectives so far. Promptly at 2am, we set off again, this time to go all the way and right through the minefields.

We still had some way to go and soon got level with the guns and saw the barrage much closer. Saw an ambulance or two coming back. There was a thick pall of dust over our minefield, which made visibility a bit difficult. We went on fairly smoothly until we were through the British minefields, but then stopped for a bit because there was some hitch in making the gaps in the German minefields. The long row of Shermans was most impressive and, as I heard afterwards, all the infantry were very cheered to see so many tanks. I told the driver and front gunner to close down their flaps because a few German shells were bursting not far away. I was the last troop in the squadron. Freddie was leading, followed by David, then Humphrey and Squadron HQ, Bill and myself – followed by C Squadron.

Everything was now OK in front and we advanced through the lights marking the first German minefield. I'd expected to see dead men lying everywhere, but saw none. Another halt before coming to the second minefield. There were now signs of very faint light in the east, and I began to wonder whether we would get through before dawn. The wireless was now working, so presumably first contact with the enemy had been made. It was a relief hearing the CO's and all the other familiar voices on the air. Presently Freddie's voice came over the air to say he could go on. More shells bursting around. Went on and the next thing that happened was that Douglas MacCallan's tank struck a mine. No damage, except the track blown off. We went round his tank and then two or three tanks in C Squadron behind me hit mines, so I was lucky to get past with my troop. There was now a hitch in front as there was another small minefield ahead, and dawn was approaching. The CO (Alex Barclay) on the air seemed to be a bit perturbed that we wouldn't get through before light. However Freddie, with a great deal of initiative, went on ahead and discovered that all was clear through the last minefield. Eventually our squadron got through and deployed as far as possible, and C Squadron behind us managed to squeeze in too. It was now getting very light. The first thing we saw was a lot of Valentines (infantry tanks) with the Australians. The situation was very confused. We were being fired on by an assortment of stuff, nobody knew from where. None of us were quite clear where the Australians were to our front, or what the Valentines were engaging. We were a long way short of where we were meant to be by dawn, chiefly because the infantry had not got all their objectives.

Eventually Humphrey moved the squadron forward through the last minefield and kept it more or less together. The position now clarified itself. A bit of high ground one mile to our left was still held by the enemy. You could see one or two German and some Italian tanks and lorries on the skyline, so we started shooting at them at very long range. We were placed awkwardly with no cover, no hull-down positions and little chance of deploying. I gazed through my binoculars at the skyline, directed the gunner onto various targets and corrected his fire. Suddenly the driver tells me we are hit in front. 'Any damage?' I ask. 'No sir.' 'Okay, continue shooting.' The driver's laconic voice again, 'Another hit, sir – showing daylight this time.' So I thought we'd better change our position a bit. We did this, and started shooting again. I'm looking out of the top when two things happen. There is a terrific clang on the front of the turret and blue sparks fly about inside (this turned out to have been a hit from a 50mm on the gun mantle) and then I get a violent blow on my left elbow. Think for a moment I'm hit. But the loader points out that my elbow was behind the gun when it recoiled – disappointing and bloody annoying. Don't think it is damaged much and continue fighting. Presently I find a small sandbank behind which there is a little cover. Ring up Humph and tell him, and he sends Freddie's troop to join me. We take the opportunity to look at the hits on the tank. The one on the front of the turret made the hell of a big dent. The two in front of the driver didn't leave much of a mark. We have a very quick brew-up of tea. That makes a lot of difference.

We still had practically all our tanks, and some of the ones that had been mined were with us again. Various reconnaissances were made and eventually about 6pm the Colonel said over the wireless that he was proposing to try and get to the objective, Point 33, that we should have been on by this morning. Humphrey seemed a bit doubtful. However, we formed up ready to advance, B Squadron right, C Squadron left. Then, all of a sudden, things began to happen. Humphrey's tank is hit, and goes up in a sheet of flame. I see him and his crew jump out and get into a trench. Humph is holding his hands over his face. Another tank in Squadron HQ goes up, and also one in C Squadron. All this is from a German tank counter-attack coming in on our left behind ourselves and the 9th Lancers. Now I got only rough impressions of what was happening. Somebody fires some smoke in front. We all follow suit. Things were looking pretty sticky. Then the Colonel's voice came over the air telling us to get over to the left – i.e. along the front of the minefield – to join the 9th. A Squadron in their Crusaders go first. We follow, as fast as we can. It seems incredibly slow. We are firing at German tanks to our right front. See one or two go up in flames. We get to the corner of the minefield, then turn, and the 9th are just in front of us. We join onto them and form a line facing the enemy. We've only lost one tank on the way. The 9th seem to have done some very good shooting. I can see several German tanks on fire in front. The remainder are holding off or withdrawing. Quite a few Italians run towards us waving anything white they can get hold of, from newspapers to vests and pants. They seem terrified out of their wits, and can't stop running. It's now getting rapidly darker and the situation is stabilized somewhat. 75mm ammunition is running low and we do a good deal of machine gunning.

Presently, when it's quite dark, we go over to our left and back a bit and prepare to leaguer for the night with the 9th. Collect B Squadron together and find we have 7 or 8 tanks. David Gay is missing. Discover afterwards that he was found wounded when an exploding shell caused his turret flap to bang down on his head. Bill's tank is hit in the petrol tank, and it looks as if he'll go back with it to the fitters. We now get settled in for the night, which promises to be uncomfortable. John Weller Poley, the artillery observer with the 9th, joins us and shares a meal with Freddie and myself, which Corporal Lean, the wireless operator, has made – tea and M&V stew, plus some whiskey which I had on board. Everybody rather gloomy and depressed, Freddie especially so.

Bad night. Machine-gun bullets whistling through the leaguer and also some bombing. Ammunition and petrol lorries arrive during the night. One of B Squadron's petrol lorries had gone up on a mine, so we had to borrow off C Squadron.

It is decided to amalgamate B and C Squadrons to form one Sherman Squadron commanded by Bill Manger, 2 i/c George Rich, troop leaders Freddie, Stephen Christie-Miller, Dick Ward and myself. I've still got my troop sergeant Weyhill and his tank with me, and my third tank is Sgt Curry from David's troop.

At first light we moved out with this organization, preceded by a troop of armoured cars and some scout cars, the intention being to advance to Point 33, our objective of yesterday morning. We advance in 'Box' formation with Freddie and Stephen leading. We'd gone about a quarter of a mile when I noticed that the armoured cars in front had stopped. Also saw the traces of 88 shells. We went on, and soon ran into trouble. The squadron came under heavy 88-fire from our left front. Freddie's tank was hit in the turret; I remember seeing bits and pieces fly into the air, and his cap jump out of the turret and fall to the ground beside the tank. Then in rapid succession the other tank in his troop and Stephen's tank were hit – also Sgt Curry in my troop. Things looked pretty grim. I remember the voice of the Colonel saying perfectly calmly, 'If you're in trouble with 88s, just put out smoke and everything will be OK.' We kept moving about and never staying still for more than a few seconds. I remember George standing on the back of his tank smoking a cigar, and discovered afterwards that he was attending to his gunner who had been wounded. Noticed that Sgt Weyhill's tank was out of action and on fire. We withdrew a little under cover of the smoke and had a look round. In reply to the Colonel, who asked if everything was now OK, Bill Manger said 'Yes, but not much left.' This was true, because out of 12 tanks we now seemed to have 4. We now stayed where we were, engaging various targets at long range. Ammunition came up later. While refilling I found Sgt Weyhill, who was shaken but OK. The rest of his crew had been killed and I discovered that the MO had also been killed that morning in his scout car.

During the rest of the day we remained in the same place. There was an Italian attack on the Australians on our right, which was repulsed with 13 tanks destroyed. In the evening the 10th Hussars attacked a ridge in front. They didn't do any good – got involved in a minefield and lost 5 tanks, destroyed by 88s. We knocked out one of the latter.

From now on things became very uninteresting as far as we were concerned.

I now take up the account of the battle from an A Squadron viewpoint.

In the morning of 24 October A Squadron was spread out in the open between two parallel enemy minefields. For hours nothing much seemed to happen. Then, in the early evening, an attack was ordered on Point 33, a barely perceptible elevation in the desert floor which gave a commanding view of an extensive swathe of ground. B and C Squadrons moved forward with A Squadron following in reserve, but they had not gone far before they were caught in a hail of fire from 88mm anti-tank guns, and several tanks were knocked out. We were ordered to change direction left, along the front of a minefield, into the area where the 9th Lancers were operating. As my tank swung left-handed I passed behind a blazing knocked-out tank with Humphrey Weld, the commander of B Squadron, huddled on the ground for shelter behind it. He suffered serious burns to his arms. We passed the tanks of the 9th Lancers forming

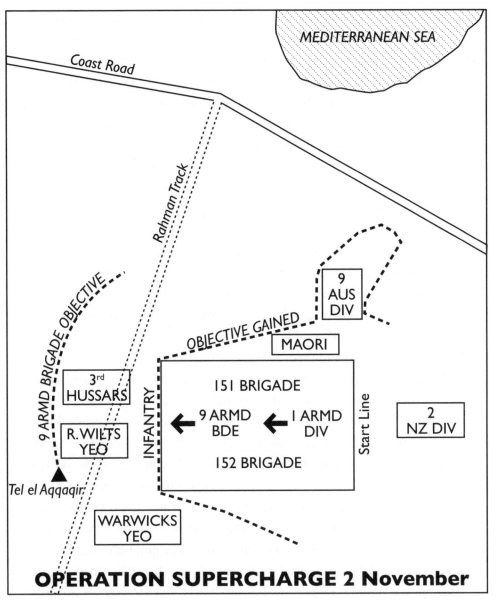

Map 3: Operation SUPERCHARGE.

up to face Point 33 and took station on their left. Immediately a score of German tanks came charging down the slope from Point 33 to be met by the fire of the 9th Lancer Shermans. Many of the enemy tanks were knocked out and the charge was halted. A knocked-out German Mark III stood a few hundred yards to my front and I kept up a steady fire from my mortar around it in case any of the crew were sheltering there. By now the light was fading fast and we leaguered for the night close by. I found an Italian trench and had a safe night's sleep inside it.

At first light the next morning B and C Squadrons were ordered to renew their attack on Point 33, but were again repelled by the fire of 88s. Freddie Barnado and Stephen Christie-Miller, two of the best and bravest troop leaders, were killed. Those who had seen him before the attack said that they could read death in Freddy's face, so terrible was his premonition. In fact the advancing tank had no chance against the dug-in 88, which was able to knock out any tank at ranges up to 3,000 yards. Attempts to capture Point 33 by the unsupported tanks of 2 Armoured Brigade had to be abandoned.

When it was fully light that morning we in A Squadron could see that we were at the southern end of a shallow bowl of desert devoid of any vestige of vegetation, bare and stony. A mile away in front of us the ground rose to a low ridge, and presently we were treated to an extraordinary sight. Moving from right to left beyond the ridge and projecting high above it at a steep angle like a gigantic rampant penis was the six-yard barrel of a huge gun mounted on an invisible tank or self-propelled vehicle. Our gunners opened fire, and by an amazing stroke of luck the very first shot not only scored a direct hit but knocked it out. The gun barrel came to an abrupt halt, and clouds of black smoke began to billow above its position. It continued to burn all day, but we were never able to discover on what kind of vehicle it was mounted.

There was little other sign of enemy movement. Obviously we were kept under observation, and my tank was the target of regular fire from an anti-tank gun at extreme range. One shot would land a few yards in front of the tank, kicking up a little plume of dust, followed shortly by another shot a few yards behind. I would then move the tank 100 yards forwards or backward to upset the range, and the process would be repeated all over again. It continued for most of the day, but they never did succeed in scoring a hit.

Scanning the empty desert bowl through my field-glasses I noticed a darker patch on the ochre desert floor that might have been a slit trench or a weapon hit. I estimated that the range was about 1,400 yards, just close enough for my mortar, and opened fire. The first shot landed just in front of and the second just behind the target, and I was preparing to fire a third which should score a hit when Jackie Harman, the second-in-command of the squadron, came on the air and said that he could see what I was aiming at, but it was beyond my reach. In fact he must have been mistaken as to my target, which was clearly within range, but I had to abandon the exercise.

That evening I was ordered to hand over my tank to another crew, go back to the echelon, take over a new tank when it was delivered, and remain in reserve. The regiment was in the line for a few more days, but saw little action, and then was withdrawn into reserve for the final push that was being planned. The original plan for a breakout by the armour had failed. The enemy defences, behind successive minefields, were deeper than had been estimated, and for days the battle settled into what Monty called the 'crumbling process' by which the enemy infantry were methodically reduced in limited attacks. The chief agents of the crumbling were the 9th Australian Division who emerged as the best infantry in the desert. Every day I walked over to regimental headquarters to study the situation map, and every day I found that the Australians had made further progress, pressing their attack northwards to threaten the coast road and cut off the German 164th Division that was holding the northernmost part of the line. It was a superb feat of arms that forced Rommel to concentrate his reserves in that part of the front and leave weakened defences farther south. That gave Monty the opportunity he had manoeuvred for and led to the launching of Operation SUPERCHARGE that finally decided the result of the battle of Second Alamein.

SUPERCHARGE consisted of an attack by the 2nd New Zealand Division with two British Infantry brigades which blew a hole 4,000 yards deep in the German defences. That was followed by an attack by 9 Armoured Brigade with the object of breaching the anti-tank defences on the Tel el Aqqaqir ridge, which would open the way for 1st Armoured Division to exploit into open country beyond. The infantry attack was a total success. The 9 Armoured Brigade attack faltered because a half-hour delay meant that, instead of getting in amongst the defences in the dark, they were silhouetted against the lightening eastern sky of early dawn. In spite of fighting with extreme gallantry, and knocking out a number of guns, their attack did not achieve its objectives. Monty had told Currie, the brigade commander, that he was prepared to accept 100 per cent casualties in the brigade – not a very sensible thing to say, because if you have 100 per cent casualties you have lost the battle.

By the time the tanks of 1st Armoured Division came up to 9 Armoured Brigade, Currie's formation had been destroyed as a fighting force. The Royal Wiltshire Yeomanry had only two 'runners' left, the 3rd Hussars seven and the Warwickshire Yeomanry eight with two more in Brigade HQ; of the original ninety-four tanks, seventy-five had been lost. Four hundred men of 9 Armoured Brigade had ridden into battle, of whom 230 had been killed or wounded. Their charge was a latter day equivalent of that of the Light Brigade at Balaclava eighty-eight years, almost to the day, earlier.

Consequently 1st Armoured Division did not have a clear path into open country. My troop was the leading troop of the leading squadron of the leading regiment of 1st Armoured Division. When my tank drew clear of the sand fog of the minefield lane I could see, far ahead, the chaotic evidence of 9 Armoured Brigade's battle. Tracer trails criss-crossed the sky, guns flashed and tanks exploded in smoke and flame. Tom Toller's troop, the next through the minefield, was to come up level with me on my right, but it seemed to take ages to appear. My left flank was clear; the 9th Lancers took care of that. It was my right flank that worried me. That side was still in pitch darkness, a sinister black wall posing an inscrutable threat. At last Tom's tank raced up alongside mine, his head and shoulders, clad in a white sheepskin Hebron coat, visible in the turret. At that moment there was a gun flash in the black wall and Tom's tank was hit. It stopped dead, and I was aware of Tom in the same instant vaulting from the turret like a jockey baling out from a falling chaser. The forward observation officer of our supporting artillery regiment, the 11th (HAC) RHA, was following the leading troop. He swung his Honey tank in the direction of the gun flash, but the next shot penetrated the front of his tank and killed him. Tom fortunately was unscathed, but his driver was killed.

The advance had come to a halt under fire from 88s on Tel el Aqqaqir, and for the next two days there was little movement. Tom Draffen had been promoted to second-in-command of a brigade, and command of the regiment had been taken over by Alex Barclay, the former commander of A Squadron. Alex was the most level-headed of commanding officers. For long periods he would be a man of few words. On one occasion after the end of the war in Africa I was sitting beside him in the ante-room waiting for the announcement of lunch. For ten minutes he was silent. Then he said, 'Peter, do you think the anti-tank gun is the master of the tank on the battlefield?' 'Yes, Colonel,' I answered. 'Oh yes, I see,' he said, and then was silent again for another five minutes. In his business dealings after the war he was a bit of a charlatan but in battle he could be relied on never to commit the regiment to some wild and ill-considered action. He was the perfect CO for the battle at Tel el Aqqaqir.

So deep was the penetration of the enemy defences by Operation SUPERCHARGE that the Tel stood as the last bastion before a total breakthrough, and the Germans had to hold us there or lose the battle. Every tank, every anti-tank gun, every field gun that they could muster was deployed against us. Shot and shell rained down on us ceaselessly and by the end of the second day my nerves, for the only time in the war, were beginning to fray. John Tatham-Warter had survived the Battle of the Gazala Line sitting with Tom Draffen on the back of their command tank. To expose himself in the same way to the far more concentrated fire at Tel el Aqqaqir was suicidally brave, and he was killed outright standing on the back of his tank to direct the squadron. He was succeeded by Jackie Harman, the only other officer that I met during the war with the same instinctive sense of what was practicable in the army. John and Jackie were both Old Wellingtonians, and A was a remarkably OW squadron, as I myself and another of the troop leaders, Peter Gill, were also educated at Wellington College.

During a rare lull in the battle a bare-headed infantryman rose from a nearby slit trench, walked over to my tank, and handed up his empty water bottle. We filled it from the spare can we carried, and before he went back to his slit trench he laid his hand on the side of the tank and said, 'You wouldn't get me in one of them fucking mobile coffins.'

The second day of the SUPERCHARGE battle, 2 November, saw Rommel's most determined counter-attack. In the heat haze of the midday sun line after line of panzers, supported by Italian tanks, hurled themselves against the front held by 2 Armoured Brigade. It led to the immolation of the 21st Panzer Division. The Shermans took a heavy toll, and when the attack was called off late in the day 117 Axis tanks had been destroyed, eleven of them by the Bays. One of them fell to George Rich, the second in command of B Squadron. Alex Barclay called him up on the radio to congratulate him. 'What was the range?' Alex asked. 'Well, it was fifteen hundred, up two turns; I don't know what that makes it,' said George in a masterly throwaway line. As far as the present battle was concerned, the 21st Panzer Division had ceased to exist as a cohesive fighting force.

The breakthrough, when it came two days later, was the result of an infantry attack farther south. As we moved round to exploit the break I passed a dead German officer sprawled on the ground, wearing a grey overcoat with a shiny pair of field-glasses round his neck. It seemed a golden opportunity to acquire some first-class field-glasses but, mindful of the German practice of booby-trapping corpses, I decided to ignore it.

The final breakthrough was on the front of the Trieste Division, which had disintegrated. Having had no word from Trieste of their rout, von Thoma, the commander of the *Afrikakorps*, went down in his command

The officers of The Bays with Her Majesty Queen Elizabeth, later the Queen Mother, 18 September 1941.

Sandhurst. The pre-war Royal Military College became an OCTU (Officer Cadet Training Unit) for the Royal Armoured Corps during the war and it was there that I reported for training as an officer in 1941.

The Bays team which won the Inter-Regimental Polo Tournament at Hurlingham in 1931. From left to right: George Fanshawe, Evelyn Fanshawe, Alex Barclay and Tom Draffen, all subsequently Commanding Officers of the regiment. The two last-named were my first two Commanding Officers.

Winston Churchill on a visit to the regiment in 1941 with the Commanding Officer, Tom Draffen.

George Streeter, regimental second-in-command at Second Alamein, in his desert dug-out.

Humphrey Weld, wounded at Second Alamein when commanding B Squadron.

John Tatham-Warter, killed at Second Alamein when commanding A Squadron.

Robert Crosbie-Dawson, awarded the MC after his Grant took nineteen hits at the Battle of the Gazala Line. Commanded A Squadron at the Battle of the Mareth Line.

The Bays' regimental badge, hand embroidered by the author's sister, Laura Watson.

Crusaders in the desert. These fast cruiser tanks were armed with a light 2-pounder gun and were mechanically unreliable.

By May 1942 the regiment included a squadron of American Grant tanks with a turret-mounted 37mm gun and a 75mm gun in a sponson on the right side.

Reconnaissance troops were equipped with the American M3 Stuart light tank, known as the Honey in British service. The Honey was fast and reliable but vulnerable to all but light anti-tank weapons. This Honey was knocked out in action against the *Afrikakorps*. (Bundesarchiv)

German 88mm anti-aircraft guns deployed in the anti-tank role during the Battle of the Gazala Line. These guns could knock out any Allied tank well beyond the range at which the Allied tanks could engage the 88s. (Bundesarchiv)

The Crusader Mark III was fitted with a 6-pounder gun but its mechanical problems were never resolved fully.

American M4 Sherman tanks began arriving in North Africa in summer 1942. Among the formations to receive the Sherman was 2 Armoured Brigade of 1st Armoured Division.

Shermans of 2 Armoured Brigade in training for Eighth Army's planned offensive.

Scramble! Tank crews mounting Shermans in haste during at an emergency in the North African Campaign.

Shermans of the Bays at El Alamein, October 1942.

Shermans of the Bays preparing to move off. The wartime censor has obliterated the 1st Armoured Divisional badge of a charging rhino from the front of the leading tank.

Second Alamein. Shermans of 2 Armoured Brigade moving up to the attack on the early morning of 24 October 1942 with an artillery barrage in the distance.

Douglas MacCallan helps replenish the ammunition of a Sherman. Don Burley, who later earned the DCM in Italy, is in the turret.

The Commonwealth War Graves Commission Cemetery at El Alamein.

The headstone of Major John Tatham-Warter MC, killed in action at El Alamein commanding A Squadron of the Bays.

MAJOR
J. DE G. TATHAM-WARTER
M.C.
THE QUEEN'S BAYS
ROYAL ARMOURED CORPS
2ND NOVEMBER 1942   AGE 27

The author in front of a Sherman at the El Alamein Museum in 2009.

German anti-tank
gun positions

Bays axis of
advance

The ground at Montecieco where the Bays launched their abortive attack on Point 153. Casa Battaglini and Point 158 are on the skyline.

Sergeant Don Burley who was awarded the Distinguished Conduct Medal for gallantry in action at Montecieco in September 1944.

Casa Battaglini
(Point 158)

The author (left) with Amadeo Montemaggi, Douglas MacCallan and Jackie Harman at the Queen's Bays' Memorial, Montecieco, 1994.

Post-war the author became involved in journalism and horse-racing, a new career which brought him into contact with many of the great names in racing.

Lavinia Duchess of Norfolk with Moon Madness, winner of the St Leger in 1986, which she bred and owned.

Reference Point, bred and owned by Louis Freedman, winning the Derby in 1987. Ridden by Steve Cauthen, he led from start to finish.

Celtic Swing, bred by Lavinia Duchess of Norfolk and trained by her daughter, Lady Herries. He was sold to Peter Savile, for whom he was a brilliant two-year-old and winner of the French Derby as a three-year-old.

Polygamy, far left, bred and owned by Louis Freedman, winning the Oaks in 1974. Dibidale, centre right, was unlucky because her saddle slipped right round underneath her belly. She gained her revenge by beating Polygamy in the Irish Oaks.

The Ever Ready Derby Stakes continued

16 REFERENCE POINT 9 st 0 lb
(B c Mill Reef (USA) – Home On The Range)
S. CAUTHEN
Owner   Mr. Louis Freedman
Trainer   H. R. A. Cecil, Newmarket
Breeder   Cliveden Stud
YELLOW, BLACK spots, YELLOW sleeves and cap.

Form   311-1

17 ROMANTIC PRINCE 9 st 0 lb
(Ch c Henbit (USA) – Supremely Royal)
W. RYAN
Owner   Mr. Ivan Allan
Trainer   C. F. Wall, Newmarket
Breeder   Mr. Ivan Allan
RED, LIGHT BLUE chevrons on body.

Form   0-014

18 SADJIYD (FR) 9 st 0 lb
(B c Labus (FR) – Stoyana (FR))
Y. SAINT-MARTIN
Owner   H.H. Aga Khan
Trainer   A. de Royer Dupre, France
Breeder   H.H. Aga Khan
GREEN, RED epaulets.

Form   1-111 D

19 SIR HARRY LEWIS (USA) 9 st 0 lb
(B c Alleged (USA) – Sue Babe (USA))
J. REID
Owner   Mr. Howard Kaskel
Trainer   B. W. Hills, Marlborough
Breeders   Mr. Joseph Allen & Regent Farm
WHITE, EMERALD GREEN hoop and cap,
hooped sleeves.

Form   2-11

20 THAMEEN (USA) 9 st 0 lb
(Ch c Nureyev (USA) – Secretarial Queen (USA))
M. HILLS
Owner   Mr. Hamdan Al-Maktoum
Trainer   J. Thomson Jones, Newmarket
Breeder   Mr. Tom Gentry
ROYAL BLUE, WHITE epaulets, striped cap.

Form   4140-14

The Ever Ready Derby Stakes continued

21 WATER BOATMAN 9 st 0 lb
(Ch c Main Reef – Sea Harrier)
B. ROUSE
Owner   Sheikh Mohammed
Trainer   B. W. Hills, Marlborough
Breeder   Mr. T. Brennan
MAROON, WHITE sleeves,
MAROON cap, WHITE star.

Form   3-302

Remember to retain all betting tickets until 'Weighed In' is announced

STANDARD TIME 2 MINS. 36 SECS.

WINNING TIME ... 2.33.9

1986: SHAHRASTANI (USA), 9-0, W. R. SWINBURN 11/2 Fav.
Owner: H.H. Aga Khan – Trainer: M. R. Stoute
17 Ran

1st ....

2nd ....

3rd ....

4th ....

TIME .... DISTANCES ....

THE EVER READY DERBY TROPHY
The presentation of the Ever Ready Derby Trophy will be made by
Sir Gordon White KBE, Chairman, Hanson Industries Inc.
in the Unsaddling Enclosure after the race.

An extract from the race card at Epsom on Derby Day, 3 June 1987.

tank to investigate, and was made prisoner by Grant Singer of the Reconnaissance Troop of the 10th Hussars. Controversially von Thoma was entertained to dinner that evening by Monty, and was informed that Singer had been killed in action that afternoon. Subsequently von Thoma wrote from captivity a letter of condolence to Singer's parents, an act of exceptional chivalry in the midst of war.

When we had driven clear of the last Axis defences we became aware of a remarkable contrast. For days we had been surrounded closely by tanks, in fighting trim or smoking wrecks, deafened by the cacophony of battle; now we had big vistas of open desert, nothing in sight but a few distant groups of vehicles, either fleeing Germans or our own armoured cars, and soundless except for the hum of our tank engines and the rattle of their tracks. We steered a north-westerly course, aiming for the coast road twenty miles west of Alamein, with A Squadron on the left and a composite squadron of the remnants of B and C Squadrons on the right. We made steady progress for a couple of hours when the composite squadron on higher ground encountered a solitary 88. No longer the terrifying organ of destruction of an organized system of defence, the 88 was disabled by the first shot from the leading Sherman. A single surviving member of the crew came running over the ridge top, within sight of A Squadron, and jumped into a deep unoccupied vehicle pit. One of our tank commanders lobbed a hand grenade from his turret. It went bouncing down the slope towards the vehicle pit, like a cricket ball over a rough outfield. The German soldier watched mesmerized, frozen in terror, one hand stretched behind him touching the wall of the pit. Yards before it reached him, the grenade exploded.

Was it the murder of an unarmed soldier? It could be argued that it was. On the other hand, the German had had the option of surrendering to the composite squadron, but had not taken it, choosing to attempt to escape and fight again another day. It was the duty of the British tankmen to foil that attempt by any means. That is the kind of unanswerable moral dilemma that happens inevitably in war, when there is no time for the consideration of alternatives.

There were several vehicle pits, and beside them a row of brown bell tents showing signs of hasty departure by the occupants. Tent flaps were open and, inside, camp furniture was upturned and paper littered everywhere. In one of them I found a stack of family photographs and pocketed them for study at my leisure. They disclosed an extraordinary anomaly. About three inches by four and taken with a cheap camera, they all showed the same scene, a terraced hillside garden with a clump of pine trees in the background. They were family pictures, of a soldier in uniform, obviously on leave, a demure looking blonde in a dirndl, an elderly couple, probably parents, sometimes sitting on a garden seat, and several younger family members. They appeared in various groupings and postures, but the same people were in all the pictures – except the last, in which only the soldier and the girl in the dirndl appeared. She was grinning inanely at the camera, while his flies were open and his erect penis jutted out, firmly grasped in her left hand, while his face was alight with erotic excitement. What had happened to the rest of the family when this scene was enacted, I wondered. The picture threw a curious light on German domestic culture.

The coast road, when we reached it an hour later, presented a spectacle of utter disorder. There was a jumble of German trucks, facing in every direction, abandoned for want of petrol. Some were empty, some had their loads intact. One contained bales of underclothes, ready no doubt for distribution as winter clothing. The tailboard was down, some of the bales had been torn open and streams of white vests and pants had cascaded down and were strewn upon the ground.

That evening the armoured cars were already on the escarpment at Fuka, forty miles west of Alamein. All formal encoding of messages was sacrificed in the interests of speed. Herbert Lumsden, the commander of X Corps, the designated *corps de chasse*, spoke on the radio to issue the order, 'I have got a cockstand tonight, and I want you to make the maximum use of that cockstand.' So the place name Fuka was incorporated for urgency's sake in an informal British army code.

November is a month of occasional rainstorms in the desert. On 7 November a persistent deluge fell on the desert between Alamein and Mersa Matruh, reducing large areas to a muddy swamp impassable by wheeled traffic. For twelve hours no petrol lorries could reach the Bays and the tanks were stranded a few miles short of their objective to cut the coast road. If the weather had stayed dry there is no doubt that we should have cut off many of the retreating Germans – not all of them, probably, because it was practically impossible to entrap an entire army when there was open desert flank. The Germans had faced and failed to solve this problem when Eighth Army was in full retreat from the Gazala Line five months earlier. The rain put an end to our part in the pursuit from Alamein.

Montgomery has been indicted by modern military historians for his alleged dilatory pursuit of the Panzerarmee after Alamein but, as far as I am concerned, the charge is false. There was no lack of urgency on the part of either Monty or Lumsden. They could not control the weather.

Two days later I encountered a group of disconsolate Italian soldiers wandering lost in the desert. They wore ragged, crumpled, filthy grey uniforms, had no arms and were wet, hungry and miserable. They were no threat to anybody. There was nothing I could do for them but point them due east and tell them to keep walking till they met some formation that could take them prisoner.

The Italians had a bad name as soldiers. They were despised and maltreated by their German allies, and regarded as a pushover by their enemies. In truth their reputation was not wholly justified. Their best troops, like the Folgore Parachute Division which fought alongside the incomparable German Ramcke Brigade at Second Alamein, deserved respect. But they had too many disadvantages to overcome. They were badly led; their field guns had nothing like the range of the British twenty-five pounder; their tanks were poorly armed and armoured; and their transport vehicles were inadequate in quality and quantity for an army fighting a twentieth-century war. Many of their trucks had solid rubber tyres, which must have given an appallingly uncomfortable ride over rough desert going and shaken the trucks themselves to pieces before many miles had been covered. Few Italian soldiers had any heart for the struggle, and that party I met after Alamein were utterly demoralized. It was impossible not to feel sympathy for them, committed to a hopeless war in pursuit of the unrealistic ambitions of the *Duce*.

Rommel's army had been comprehensively defeated. With his rear threatened by the Allied landings in Algeria, he had no choice but to fight occasional delaying actions at least until he reached the region of the Tunisian border with Libya. Until then there was no active role for the Bays to play.

Second Alamein was a triumph for Monty's strategy and tactics. Alexander, who had replaced Auchinleck as Commander-in-Chief Middle East and was Monty's boss, left the organization and conduct of the battle to him, and Monty's inspirational charisma, meticulous planning, use of massed artillery, ability to conjure up reserves for deployment at vital times and places, and unshakeable self-confidence were essential ingredients in his success. His one weakness was his failure to grasp the limitations of armour when there is rough parity in the quality of tanks and anti-tank guns, as there was at Second Alamein. Where parity exists the tank is more effective in defence than in attack, as was demonstrated by the destruction of the panzers at Tel el Aqqaqir when our tanks fought a defensive battle, and the gallant action of 2nd Rifle Brigade at *Snipe*, where fifty-seven Axis tanks and self-propelled guns were accounted for by 6-pounder anti-tank guns. The initial plan for an armoured breakthrough was unrealistic in the circumstances, and this shortcoming was compounded by a serious underestimate of the depth of the German minefields. This failing of the army commander did not count for much once Second Alamein had been won, and the war in Africa proceeded to its inevitable end.

Chapter Seven

The End in Africa

The winter of 1942–43, following Alamein, is mostly a blur in my memory. The regiment was not involved in the pursuit of Rommel's beaten army to Tripoli and beyond, and I am indebted to Willy Beddington's *History of The Queen's Bays* for an outline of those months. By mid-November the regiment was halted at Acroma, on the escarpment a few miles west of Tobruk, where most of the Shermans were handed over to 22 Armoured Brigade for use in the pursuit. The *History* relates:

> The next day they [the regiment] moved on again up the coast road as far as the two to three shacks which made up the township of Tmimi, where they turned off up the Segnali track and, after going on another ten miles into the desert, set up their leaguer. This piece of desert was to be their home for the next three and a half months. … Courses, leaves and local recreation were arranged … . The ground was levelled to make football and hockey grounds; lights and wireless sets were run off the tank batteries … and so some degree of civilization and healthy activity was improvised to occupy the minds and absorb the energies of the troops in the spare moments of the day and the earlier darkness of winter nights in the desert.

Even by the high standards of the Libyan desert the surroundings of the camp were singularly bleak, featureless and uninviting. The monotonous grey flatness of the outlook was relieved just once. In the middle of January a heavy rainstorm of the same magnitude as the 7 November downpour hit the area; but whereas the November deluge had been followed by days of low, leaden skies and the desert remained a muddy wasteland, the January deluge gave way to sunshine and warm hours of daylight. Within forty-eight hours millions of tiny flowers had sprung through the sandy desert surface, carpeting the ground as far as the eye could see in a kaleidoscope of yellow, purple and red. The latest-joined troop leader, John (Cushy) North, a keen horticulturalist who ran a chrysanthemum farm in Sussex after the war, dug up some of the plants and arranged them on the middle of the A Squadron mess table, a large wooden sign taken from the roadside. Assiduously tended, they lasted longer than the myriads left in the ground outside, which died and disappeared within a few days.

Once I went on a foraging expedition to Benghazi. We found a line of Bedouin shepherds squatting on the ground under the town walls, but all they had to sell was sheeps' testicles. However, we did unearth a hoard of Italian army ration tins of peas and beans which turned out to be surprisingly succulent and tasty, especially the beans. My only other outing was with a party of about twenty officers from the Bays, 9th Lancers, and 10th Hussars to the battlefield of Antelat, Saunnu and 'Well with Windpump' where 2 Armoured Brigade had suffered the disastrous rout a year earlier which precipitated the Msus Stakes. At various points officers from each regiment gave accounts of their part in the battle, but no fresh wisdom emerged apart from a consensus that the 'in and out', the conventional attacking manoeuvre of the time by which a squadron of tanks would charge the enemy on a diagonal course, turn through an angle of 90 degrees and speed away again, firing furiously in each leg of the manoeuvre, was futile and courting disaster. It no longer figured in the tank commander's repertoire.

It's a long, long way - 1,150 miles - from Mersa Matruh to Mareth, where the 1st Armoured Division, and more importantly from my point of view, The Queen's Bays, were to fight their next battle. The narrow ribbon of metalled road that connected those two points took a detour through the Djebel Akhdar – the Green Mountain – in the hump of Cyrenaica, where the model villages built for Italian colonists stood deserted in the winter of 1942-43, and the fertile fields were untilled. From the slopes where the road descended from the western end of the Djebel to the cultivated coastal belt that extended for 130 miles east of Tripoli, there was not a sign of greenery of any kind. A character in an Oscar Wilde story complained that 'Nature was badly lighted and too green'. For many miles along the sun-baked coast of Tripolitania Nature was extremely well lit and not green at all.

It was a long, long time from 7 November 1942, when the regiment disengaged from the pursuit after El Alamein, to 13 March 1943, when the regiment arrived at a halting place near Medenine, a pre-war French garrison town, ten miles short of the Mareth Line close to the Libyan-Tunisian border. The Bays had not been completely divorced from the progress of the war during these months. Jack Dallas, one of the liveliest and most amusing characters in the regiment, was attached to Army Headquarters as a Liaison Officer (LO) for the duration of the pursuit to Tripoli. Late one evening he was summoned to the army commander's presence. Monty appeared at the top of the steps of his caravan and told him in crisp, clipped tones, 'I want you to find General Wimberley and give him this message. He is to push on with the utmost urgency, speed is absolutely essential.' Douglas Wimberley was in command of the 51st (Highland) Division, which was then in the lead about 100 miles short of Tripoli. After a long search Jack located Wimberley in the small hours of a bright moonlit night. He was at the bottom of a deep wadi, with his shoulder to the tailboard of a 3-ton lorry, helping push it out of a drift of soft sand. Jack stood at the top of the bank, saluted and said, 'The army commander sends his compliments, sir. You are to push on with the utmost urgency, speed is absolutely essential.' Without relaxing his efforts Wimberley half-turned and said breathlessly over his shoulder, 'Well, you can tell the army commander that I am doing my best.'

Near Medenine the regiment was encamped on a grassy plain that stretched for ten miles to the foot of the Matmata mountains and the Mareth Line. A few days earlier it had been the site of an Axis counter-attack intended to delay any attempt to break through the Mareth Line.

Eighth Army was ready for it and an anti-tank gun screen that included the new 17-pounder guns, which could destroy any German tank, had been deployed. The result of the Battle of Medenine showed that Rommel was as oblivious as Monty of the limitations of tanks when opposed to dug-in, carefully sited anti-tank guns and tanks equal to his own. The attack was defeated with 10th, 15th and 21st Panzer Divisions suffering terribly, losing fifty tanks. Eighth Army lost none.

The Mareth Line was the strongest defensive position between El Alamein and Tunisia. Built by the French against a possible invasion from Italian Libya, it filled the fifteen-mile gap between the sea and the rugged Matmata mountains and was based on the deep and muddy Wadi Zigzaou which formed an effective anti-tank ditch. It consisted of concrete reinforced emplacements and weapon pits, sited in depth and virtually impervious to field artillery fire. The flat plain was broken only by an isolated mountain 2,000 feet high, nicknamed by the British 'Edinburgh Castle', which dominated the whole area. To get a view of the approaches to the Mareth Line, where we were expecting to fight, one afternoon Jackie Harman and I decided to walk to the top of Edinburgh Castle. A single narrow path wound through rocky outcrops and crevices to the summit, and when we were about two-thirds of the way up we saw, to our horror, Montgomery, accompanied by an ADC and a staff captain, approaching us on their way down. We were fearful that he would ask us all sorts of embarrassing questions, but there was no avoiding him; on our left there was a vertical rock-face, and on our right a sheer drop of several hundred feet. He greeted us with a cheery 'Good afternoon, gentlemen,' and then asked how long we had been in the Middle East. We told him sixteen months. 'That's not long,' he said, 'Won't send you home when this lot's over. Leave you out here to get on with it.' That was the end of the conversation. He was wrong about Jackie, who was sent home soon after the war in Africa finished two months later.

The battle of the Mareth Line opened on the night of 20 March with the now customary artillery bombardment followed by an infantry attack. The original plan was for the infantry to blow a hole in the line for the

1st Armoured Division, including the Bays, to pass through and fan out in the open country beyond. The infantry successfully penetrated the defences, but their supporting tanks and towed anti-tank guns bogged down in the Wadi Zigzaou and were picked off by enfilade fire. The infantry were then heavily counter-attacked by German tanks and their forward positions became untenable. It seemed that the Mareth Line was impregnable to frontal attack. Monty immediately accepted that this was so, and decided to switch the weight of his attack to a left hook round the west side of the Matmata mountains. The change of plan involved a very long march for 2 Armoured Brigade and the Bays, through a gap in the mountains and then north-westwards for forty miles to the area where 2nd New Zealand Division was already confronting a secondary defensive line and 21st Panzer Division.

For many miles the going was appalling, the worst we had encountered in the desert. The route crossed a seemingly endless succession of dunes bound by tussocks of coarse grass, and progress was slowed to a walking pace. It took thirteen hours to cover forty-three miles before we leaguered for the night. There were still another thirty miles to go before we reached the forming-up place for the attack, but the going had improved considerably.

The attack went in late in the afternoon of 26 March. It was led by two brigades of the New Zealand Division with 8 Armoured Brigade, and was launched from the remains of an ancient Roman wall which stretched from a lower range of hills, the Djebel Tebaga, in the west to the Matmata mountains in the east. It was supported by a concentrated effort by the Desert Air Force, whose Hurricanes, Tomahawks and Spitfires poured a rain of bombs and bullets on the German positions. They flew in with a crescendo of sound so low over our waiting tanks that it almost seemed as if they would snap off the tanks' wireless aerials. At 5.30pm it was reported that the New Zealanders had reached their objectives and it was the turn of 2 Armoured Brigade to move through and take up the advance. The light was beginning to fade and the land was suffused with a red glow from the setting sun. At first opposition was desultory. Before long we came to the lip of a narrow valley and at the bottom of it we could see, about 100 yards in front of us, the guns of a field artillery battery with piles of unfired shells stacked beside them and the bareheaded crews standing by. Our appearance took them entirely by surprise. They obviously had no idea how deeply the New Zealand attack had penetrated and surrendered without offering the slightest resistance. Two hundred and fifty German prisoners were marched to the rear. We halted as darkness fell and waited for two hours till the moon came up. The advance then continued, the 9th Lancers on the right and the Bays on the left of a north-south road leading to the oasis village of El Hamma, our objective ten miles ahead of our start point. Confusion reigned in the German ranks. From time to time single vehicles dashed past us, bouncing recklessly over the rough terrain in the half light of the moon in a desperate attempt to escape. One of the A Squadron troop leaders, Peter Gill, managed to intercept and capture a huge 210mm gun. As we drew closer to El Hamma opposition began to stiffen. Several tanks and an 88 barred the way, and in trying to take cover one of B Squadron's tanks veered off the road and subsided in a ditch, where it attracted intermittent enemy fire. I was in the leading tank of A Squadron on the left of the regiment in a curious stretch of country dotted with solid earth mounds about the height of a tank. At one moment a furiously driven German truck rattled past me, swerving round the mounds so fast that it was out of sight before I could traverse my tank's machine gun to fire at it. Five hundred yards ahead I could see the dim outline of the stone wall of El Hamma and the belt of trees beyond it encircling the village. Enfilade fire from the tanks and guns holding up the regiment on the road made further progress impossible. At 4.30am we received the order to halt until daylight.

Lieutenant General Brian Horrocks, in command of X Corps which carried out the attack, wrote in his memoirs *A Full Life*:

It was the most exciting and worrying night of my life. As my small tactical HQ consisting of three tanks took its position in the armoured mass, I realized very well that if the attack went wrong there was no doubt as to whose head would be on the block.

It worked. An armoured night attack was novel and took the Germans completely off balance. The valley through which the British armour passed would have made a perfect site for an ambush in daylight. The Germans never expected a night attack, especially with armour in addition.

Although we had failed to take our final objective, El Hamma, the extraordinarily bold and innovative night advance of the Bays and the 9th Lancers had been successful in turning the flank of the Mareth Line and forcing the Axis forces to abandon it. A strong flank guard had been thrown out at El Hamma while the garrison of the Mareth Line poured back through the so-called Gabes Gap, a ten-mile wide space between the sea and the impassable salt marsh of the Chott Djerid which contained the Tripoli to Tunis coast road and a stretch of firm going. The course of our night advance was strewn with the destroyed hulks of German tanks and transport. One burnt-out truck presented a gruesome sight. The tailboard was down, and one crew member had been caught by the flames as he tried to escape. He seemed to be leaning on his elbows, half in and half out of the truck. He was terribly burnt. All of his clothes and his legs had been incinerated, nothing remained of them, and his head and torso reduced to pink shapelessness like a mass of partially modelled plasticine.

The next German stand was on a mountain range a few miles north of the Gabes Gap. The steepness of the mountains and the depth and sheer sides of the Wadi Akarit that formed a natural anti-tank ditch in front of them made the Bays unemployable in the battle to breach them. It was work for the Gurkhas of 4th Indian Division, who fought a brilliant night battle in which they put their kukris to devastating use. The Bays were involved in the subsequent pursuit northwards, passing through mile after mile of olive groves in the hinterland of the ports of Sousse and Sfax.

The North African campaign was nearing its end. Rommel had been recalled to Germany, a sick and disillusioned man. First Italian Army and Fifth Panzer Army were being squeezed into an ever decreasing corner of Tunisia by the offensives of the Eighth Army from the south and First

Map 4: Italy (general).

British Army and the Americans from the west. The final blow was to be struck on the First Army front with an attack straight down the main road from Medjez el Bab (the Key to the Gate) to Tunis, though the three formations transferred from Eighth Army (4th Indian Division, 7th Armoured Division and 200 Guards Brigade) were to take part and it was to be commanded by an Eighth Army general, Brian Horrocks. The attack went in on 6 May, sliced through the German defences, and the armoured cars leading the advance were in Tunis thirty-six hours later.

In the meantime, 2 Armoured Brigade with the Bays was closing up to the base of the Cap Bon peninsula, a promontory twenty miles long and five wide which jutted like a big toe into the Mediterranean from the coastline a short way east of Tunis. We were on a lush plain of vineyards, citrus orchards, copses of deciduous trees and small agricultural villages. There was some resistance and 88mm fire from one of the larger villages, Creteville, but this was soon overcome by an advance by my troop of A Squadron from the south and a squadron of our attached motorized infantry, the Yorkshire Dragoons, from the west. Ahead the mountains of the Cape Bon peninsula looked a formidable obstacle. In one of his famous orders of the day Monty had promised that 'with faith in God and in the justice of our cause … we will make the Germans face a first class Dunkirk on the beaches of Tunis'. But the Germans, ammunition spent and petrol supplies running dry, preferred surrender to the hazards of evacuation or defence of a final mountain stronghold. On 13 May the campaign in Africa was officially declared ended.

German and Italian prisoners, some packed into trucks and others on foot, came in in droves. In my tank parked by the side of the road from Cape Bon, I watched them stream past to the rear. The most surprising sight was a battalion of the elite Hermann Göring Division. Magnificent physical specimens all over six-foot tall, they had discarded their helmets and their blond hair gleamed in the sunshine. With chests thrust out and heads erect, they marched in perfect order, pride undimmed, rank after rank into captivity.

Chapter Eight

Interim Days

The end of the war in North Africa heralded a long period of relative inaction for The Queen's Bays – from 13 May 1943, the date of the German–Italian surrender in Tunisia, to 24 May 1944, when the regiment embarked on the *Durban Castle* for the voyage to Naples and the Italian campaign.

Much of the summer of 1943 was spent at Olivettia, a pleasant area of fertile irrigated land twenty miles west of Tripoli. There were olive groves, shady avenues and meadows, flooded each evening, where animal fodder was grown. The drawback was that it was terribly hot and humid, with midday temperatures rising to well over 100 degrees F. The discomfort was compounded by a *khamsin*, the hot desert wind, which blew for a week, filling the air with a scorching fog of dust and sand and rendering any metal object, even knives and forks in the shade of the mess tent, almost too hot to touch. In the afternoons we sought relief by walking down a sandy track half a mile to the sea, where a flat ledge of rock overlooked a deep pool of crystal-clear water. Half a dozen of us would dive into the pool at intervals to cool off and wash the sand out of our hair. At four o'clock the mess truck would arrive with tea and sandwiches.

While we were at Olivettia a divisional revue was organized at a theatre in Tripoli. There were sketches, comic dances, songs – all the ingredients of a revue on the London stage. Quite an array of histrionic talent was unearthed among the ranks of 1st Armoured Division. One amateur lyricist composed a musical sketch featuring the promiscuous wife of an army officer in Cairo during the desert campaigns, entitled *Scatterbrain*:

In my poor little scatterbrain head
There is only one thought, and that's bed.
When my husband's away
Keeping Hitler at bay,
I have lots of engagements to fill in the day.

She rustles the pages of her diary with one hand, then claps the other hand to her forehead in a gesture of despair:

What! Lunch at the Bristol
With Brigadier Crystal.
Oh! My poor little scatterbrain head.

Corny humour was abundant. One sketch featured a doctor's surgery. A medical orderly was seated at a table, shuffling papers. Enter a captain doctor, who asked the orderly 'Any interesting cases today?' 'Well, I saw a case of beer being carried into the officers' mess this morning,' the orderly replied. An inert figure was brought in on a stretcher, face deathly white with applied chalk. A piece of string protruded from the breast pocket of the corpse's battledress. The orderly proceeded to pull out the string, yard after yard after yard of it, until it finally came to an end tied to a condom. 'Ah, just my size,' said the orderly.

It was all applauded enthusiastically by the entertainment–starved audience.

My next move was to Medjez el Bab, a much fought–over small town on the Medjerda river, forty miles west of Tunis. In company with another A Squadron officer, Colin Munro, I was to take charge of a prisoner of war camp and 7,000 Italian soldiers. There was no danger of the prisoners trying to escape; they were happy to remain in custody and be fed while awaiting repatriation. The challenge was to ensure that they took their daily issue of a Mepacrine tablet, as the area was mosquito infested and highly malarial. The task was impossible. We could see that the tablets were issued, but their bitter taste was disgusting, and whether they were ever actually swallowed was another matter. I had known Colin Munro slightly before he joined the regiment in August 1942. We had been at Wellington together, though in different years and houses. He had been in the rackets eight, and rackets was an expensive game, so rackets players were marked down as the sons of rich parents. Colin was the son of a distinguished banker, Sir Gordon Munro. I assumed that Colin was destined for a place in fashionable London society and a lucrative job in the City after the war. Instead he emigrated to Tasmania and grew apples. Colin and I got on very well at Medjez and spent most of the time playing consequences under our mosquito nets.

My stay at Medjez did not last long. After a few days I began to feel increasingly sick and liverish, and when my urine turned black I knew that I had the so called officers' disease, jaundice. I was sent to hospital at Souk Ahras, a market town 150 miles to the west, still in the Medjerda valley, but much higher and cooler. The hospital was in a former monastery, and officers were accommodated in the monks' cells, tiny rooms into which two beds fitted neatly with a narrow space in between. My fellow patient was a 10th Hussar lieutenant called Pereina who was suffering from a chronic form of malaria in which his temperature obstinately remained two degrees above normal and defied all attempts to reduce it. He was sunk in depression and talked very little.

Not that I was in the mood for conversation for the next two weeks. I felt so ill that all I could do was lie on my side facing the white cell wall, miserable and praying for release in death. All we had to eat was tinned grade-3 salmon, but that did not matter because I had no appetite at all. We were looked after by Nurse Mills, a small woman in her late twenties, good looking in a way without being in the least sexy or attractive. She had blonde hair done in tight curls over her ears, and was bossy, cold, severe, humourless and immaculate in her blue nurse's uniform. She tried continually to spur us into some kind of activity, but we were far too ill to respond until one morning I woke up completely and miraculously cured. From feeling so sick that any thought of food revolted me, I was ravenously hungry. I longed for a big breakfast of bacon and eggs, but instead was kept in bed on a diet of grade-3 salmon.

My jaundice might be better, but in the days that followed I was faced with a new, degrading horror – crabs. I felt something crawling in my bush, and on investigating found many tiny black lice on the hairs and skin. The classic way of catching crabs is through sexual contact with an infected prostitute, but as I had had no sexual contact with a prostitute, or anyone else, the source of my infestation remained a mystery. I was terrified that some medical examination to which I might be subjected would reveal my embarrassing and humiliating condition, so I set about trying to rid myself of the invaders. Each day I went down to the showers and picked off the lice one by one and washed them down the drain. Once I gave a momentary guffaw as I remembered the character in Buck Mulligan's play in *Ulysses* – 'Crab (a bushranger).' But it really was not funny. Every day there was a fresh army of crabs. Finally, in despair, I took my razor down to the shower and shaved off my bush, subsequently removing any remaining numbers of the loathsome creatures from my scrotum and lower abdomen. That did the trick. At last I was free of crabs.

After a few more days I was given permission to go out for short walks and get some fresh air. The monastery was situated on a hill outside the town, and a few minutes' walk away there was a cafe where I could sit drinking a concoction made from crushed pomegranates and look down on the busy streets of Souk Ahras. The French owners of the cafe told me that jaundice was endemic in the region, and that nobody there observed any restriction on diet or drinking after recovering from the disease. So I ignored the instruction I received from the army doctors to abstain from alcohol for four months, and came to no harm as a result.

Poor Pereina was getting no better. Every day a doctor came in to examine him, and shook his head sadly when he found his temperature still up. One day a bevy of doctors came in and, after consultation, gave their verdict: he was making no progress, and would have a better chance of recovery if he was sent to a newly opened convalescent camp by the sea at Carthage. He, with several others, would be taken there by truck the next day.

The next morning Pereina was obviously worse. He was a sickly yellow colour and could hardly raise his head from the pillow. Nurse Mills was at her bossiest, bustling in and out of the room, forcing Pereina out of bed although he could hardly stand, nagging him to get dressed and pack his scanty belongings in his suitcase. 'Hurry,' she said. 'The truck is at the door. You are keeping everybody waiting.' I decided it was time to intervene. 'I suppose you realize he is not fit to travel,' I told her. Nurse Mills turned on me in fury. 'How dare you interfere? It is gross impertinence. Of course he is fit to travel. The doctors saw him yesterday and made all the arrangements,' she fired at me, and chivvied Pereina out of the room. Moments later the sound of a crashing body came from the passage and, after a short delay, two orderlies carried the unconscious form of Pereina back into the room and laid him on his bed.

Nurse Mills made no comment and never looked me in the eye again. A few days later I was discharged and went back to the regiment, leaving Pereina where he had been when I arrived, with no apparent prospect of recovery.

The regiment had moved to the vicinity of Boufarik, a small town with a tree lined main street twenty miles south of Algiers. Boufarik was on the edge of a dead flat semi-circular plain ringed by forested mountains. The plain was extremely fertile, filled with dense groves of orange, lemon and grapefruit trees. The local French farmers seemed to be well off at the time, living off their own produce and enjoying frequent wild boar hunts in the forests. But they were pessimistic about the future. 'When this war is over and you have gone the rebels will come down out of the mountains and murder us all,' they told us. This dire prediction was largely fulfilled in the civil war which preceded Algerian independence in 1962.

A Squadron Officers' Mess was established in a sturdily built pebbledashed single-storey farmhouse with a veranda overlooking a clearing shaded by lofty pine trees. The Squadron office was five minutes' walk away past an orchard where one could pluck a ripe orange, peel and eat the luscious fruit before reaching the office. Militarily the principal event was that our long marriage to the hapless and fallible Crusader came to an end and we were equipped with Shermans like the rest of the regiment. The crews were kept reasonably busy training on the new tanks. Jackie Harman and I applied ourselves to developing a method of indirect fire from tanks, so that in a period of static warfare the tanks could be used as supplementary artillery. With a tank planted on a flat field in the plain, we used prominent trees on the mountainside as our target. It was an absorbing exercise, but we were never allowed to employ indirect fire or a map shoot in action because the authorities claimed that they would impose excessive wear and tear on the tank guns. Jackie was soon taken from us, sent back to England to be an instructor at the RAC OCTU at Sandhurst.

Jimmy Dance was appointed to command A Squadron. Jimmy was essentially a playboy, and his military qualifications were slight. One Saturday morning before we left Marlborough two car loads of us went down to a pub in Hungerford for a drink. One car was driven by Jimmy's rather formidable wife Anne, and the passengers were Jimmy, a very pretty girl who must have been some officer's sister or daughter, Anne's Sealyham and myself. The pub car park was on the far side of a main road. The rest of us got out of the car while Anne parked it, and the Sealyham darted round in circles, lifting its leg ubiquitously and getting closer and closer to the road. Anne wound down the window and called to Jimmy, 'Look out for the little darling,' 'Oh yes,' said Jimmy, clutching the pretty girl round the waist. 'Not the girl, the dog you bloody fool,' shouted Anne in a furious tone. Jimmy's appointment to command did not augur well for A Squadron, but for the seven months we spent at Boufarik his soldierly limitations did not matter much.

Boufarik was the scene of the liveliest social round we had enjoyed since leaving England. The mainspring of this change was the presence of a 'Wrennery', a unit of well-educated WRNS cypher clerk officers, attached to naval headquarters in Algiers. The Wrens were welcome female company for the many drinks' parties and dances hosted by the regiments of 2 Armoured Brigade during the winter. Some of them were very attractive girls about twenty years old, their looks shown off by their uniforms of dark blue skirt, white blouse and blue tie. It was not unknown for romance to blossom.

One Sunday we were holding a pre-lunch drinks party at the A Squadron Mess. It was a sparkling day, with sunlight filtering down through the tops of the pines. James Weatherby, a captain in the 10th Hussars, was playing the piano. James was a member of the family that provided the top ranks of the civil service of horseracing for over two hundred years and played a vital role in the evolution of the Thoroughbred through their ownership of the *General Stud Book*; he had the precious gift of being able to play any well-known tune from memory, and he was at the top of his form that morning. I was sitting with Dick Toller, a major in the 10th Hussars, on a bench at the foot of the veranda steps. On the opposite side of the clearing, sitting on another bench, were three Wrens, of whom the middle one was a beautiful dark-haired girl. Dick was entranced. 'That's the loveliest girl I've ever seen,' he kept repeating. After he had repeated it about ten times I told him, 'Dick, if you really believe that, you must go and do something about it.' And he did. Her name was Diana Chaworth-Musters, and two months later they were married in the Anglican Church in Algiers.

Dick Toller was not the only friend of mine to marry an Algiers Wren. Another was Douglas MacCallan, who had been a year junior to me at our prep school, Parkfield, at Haywards Heath, and was in the Bays. He met and afterwards married Patricia O'Neill, an Irish girl from Ulster and a strikingly pretty blonde. It might have been supposed that these two marriages, founded in a totally alien and artificial environment, would have been fated to be of short duration. Instead they were two of the most enduring happy marriages I have known, and they remained as utterly devoted couples, and among my greatest friends, until they were parted by death more than half a century later.

I had one lucky escape. I was dicing (driving fast and recklessly) in a jeep along one of the minor metalled roads in the valley on my way to join the crew of a tank that had sunk into a deep ditch when I came upon a place where tanks, turning onto the road, had gouged deep ruts in the surface. There was no time to brake and I hit the ruts at speed. The jeep took off, spiralling high in the air, over the roadside ditch, turning a complete somersault before landing upside down in the adjacent field. Fortunately the hood was up and the struts withstood the impact of the crash. If the hood had been down or the struts had given way I should have been crushed and killed.

When I had sorted myself out I found that I had sprained my right thumb.

There were several heavy downpours and some of the nights were cold, but most of the days in Algeria were sunny and warm, and a good deal of cricket was played on makeshift pitches. There were several players of first-class standard in the 1st Armoured Division: A. G. Hazelrigg, who opened the innings for Leicestershire; Eddie Watts, a useful journeyman fast-medium bowler for Surrey who had good stories of difficulties of batting against the great Australian bowler O'Reilly; David Steel, who afterwards became Chairman of BP; and David Gay, a Bays subaltern who won an MC for gallantry in Italy. David bowled accurate fast-medium off the wrong foot and played a few games for Sussex after the war before emigrating to New Zealand to pursue a career as a schoolmaster. Most of the players were of more modest cricketing ability like Daniel Asquith, who had succeeded Alex Barclay as Bays' commanding officer. He was a stubborn left-handed bat whom even Eddie Watts, bowling at reduced pace, had difficulty in dislodging.

Track mileage was severely restricted to save wear and tear on the tanks, so only one big exercise was performed that winter. That involved loading the tanks on transporters and taking them eighty miles south over the northern range of the Atlas Mountains to a stretch of empty desert near the desert track junction of Sidi Aissa. It was bitterly cold in the mountains. We passed a desolate place called Aumale which looked like a typical Foreign Legion town. It was enclosed by high stone walls without a sign of foliage, and as we passed on the road above it we looked down on a narrow, wet cobbled street with sleet slanting across it. Snow was falling on the bare desert plain when we arrived at Sidi Aissa. The scene was thoroughly inhospitable. The exercise, in which the whole 2 Armoured Brigade took part, had no memorable feature, but we did have the opportunity to visit the oasis town of Bou Saada forty miles farther into the Sahara. Palm fronds rose high above the town walls and the air was filled with the endless cackling of thousands of chickens. There was no shortage of eggs. Bou Saada had been a tourist destination in peacetime – the town stood at the head of the Ouled Nail, which was famous for the beauty of its dancing girls – and the hotel chef was pleased to demonstrate his skill by cooking a fifty-egg omelette for twenty of us.

We had four comfortable days on the *Durban Castle* for the journey from Algiers to Naples. Someone organized a game of 'Chemmy' (Chemin-de-Fer) in the evenings after dinner. I had never played the game before, but I had £140 left in my bank account in Cairo and, reckoning that it would take a long time to get it transferred to my account in England, I decided to risk it. I lost it all in three-quarters of an hour, and have never played Chemmy again, concentrating first on poker and later on bridge instead. We sailed into the Bay of Naples at dawn, and through the porthole of the cabin I was sharing with George Rich, I could see the Isle of Capri silhouetted against the early morning sky. George, an expert horseman and keen hunting man with the Shire packs who lived at the Leicestershire village of Hillmorton, was still asleep in his bunk. I shook him awake. 'Get up, George. We're passing Capri, the most romantic island in the world.' He got up reluctantly, stumbled to the porthole, took a brief look and then turned back to his bunk, murmuring grumpily, 'Give me Hillmorton.'

Chapter Nine

Approach to War in Italy

On landing at Naples we marched to a transit camp at Afragola on the outskirts of the city. The Allied armies were advancing fast more than a hundred miles to the north, and Rome was to be liberated a few days later. In Naples the local economy and food distribution had broken down, and hordes of starving women and children descended on the waste bins on the perimeter of the camp, dressed in rags, and fighting, swearing, screaming, and cramming every scrap of waste food they could scrounge from the bins into their mouths. Twenty-four-hour armed guards had to hold them back from the camp food store. It was distressing to see human beings so stripped by hunger of all dignity and self-respect. It was a relief when, after six days, we were moved to Matera, thirty-five miles equidistant from the ports of Bari on the heel and Taranto on the instep of Italy.

Not that Matera was any paradise. It had a picturesque position on the lip of a precipitous ravine, which we overlooked from our camp outside the town. But the town infrastructure was non-existent. There was no main drainage or refuse collection, and waste of every kind was simply tipped into the ravine. Many of the habitations were caves and the whole town, from its hilltop cathedral to the ramshackle houses on the lower slopes, looked at if it might slide over the edge at any moment. There seemed to be little life on the narrow streets – just an occasional file of screeching children led by a biretta-ed priest. In modern times Matera has been re-invented as an attractive tourist destination and a World Heritage site, but in 1944 it was a scene of deprivation and squalor.

After a short stay at Matera the regiment moved ten miles north west to the area of the neighbouring towns of Gravina and Altamura where the undulating countryside provided more scope for practising the infantry and armour co-operation which was a tactical necessity in a country of mountains and fast-flowing rivers and where the wide outflanking movement and independent armoured manoeuvres of desert warfare were impossible. In the series of exercises that were undertaken at Gravina the three squadrons took it in turn to act the parts of infantry and armour, but my part in these exercises was cut short when I caught a respiratory infection. One morning as A Squadron was supposed to be infantry attacking a hill I found myself getting increasingly short of breath, and by the time I had struggled to the summit I was panting painfully. I just managed to walk back to the mess, and when I got there I was running a high temperature and collapsed on my bed. The regimental medical officer, Steve Conway, was the perfect man to have to give first aid to casualties in battle, exceptionally brave and always positioned close behind the leading troops, but his medical expertise was limited. My condition baffled him, so he despatched me to the army hospital in Bari with a note: 'Undiagnosed Fever'. But when I reached hospital hours later my temperature had miraculously subsided and I was breathing normally. The doctor who saw me was amused. 'Well,' he said, 'you've come all this way so you'd better have a comfortable night in bed here, and we'll send you back in the morning.'

I was shown to a large ward overlooking the sea, undressed and got into bed. Presently another patient walked in. He was a captain in an infantry regiment, tall and fresh-faced with a black pencil moustache, brisk in his movements. He unpacked his belongings, undressed, put on his pyjamas and got into bed, all as calmly as if he were preparing for a siesta at home. I wondered what, if anything, could be the matter with him. Half an hour later I knew. First he began to sweat, and then to shake, and then to shake more and more violently. Nurses piled blankets on top of him, but he continued to shake until the iron bedstead was rattling like a machine gun. The fit lasted half the night, until, in the small hours, it finally passed and he lay, inert and exhausted. This was malaria of an extreme type, infinitely more violent than the type from which Pereina had suffered at Souk Ahras.

From Bari I was despatched on a special duty, to guard a regiment of dummy tanks, wooden frameworks covered in canvas in the rough shape of a Sherman, set up on some low scrubby hills forty miles inland. I took with me twenty men from the Bays, and was joined by Kenneth Hedley with the same number of men from his regiment, the 4th Hussars. Our task was to maintain a chain of sentries round the dummies to prevent anyone getting close enough to see what they were – dummies – so as to pass back the information to the Germans. The duty was light. Twice a day, morning and evening, we walked round the dummy tank park perimeter to make sure that the sentries were in place and awake, saw that the men were fed and received their due share of canteen goods, and otherwise had the day to ourselves.

We had one huge stroke of luck. We came across a well-stocked NAAFI (Navy, Army and Air Force Institutes) store, apparently with a small customer base in the area and therefore able to supply us liberally with beer, chocolate and cigarettes, which kept the men happy; and they also had a case of first-class Fino sherry of which Kenneth and I bought several bottles.

Kenneth was a most entertaining companion. He was a keen mimic, a talent which he exercised at the expense of several members of his regiment. He was well-read, a hard-hitting left-handed batsman, solved *The Times*' crossword regularly and was a skilful bridge player. His weakness was an addiction to gambling. After the war he became for a time a regular visitor to English racecourses, enjoying a golden few weeks when he could do no wrong and began to think that backing winners was easy. Inevitably his winning streak came to an end and he finished with humiliating losses, greatly to the distress of his serious-minded father, a leading gynaecologist who thought horseracing was an invention of the devil and abhorred all forms of gambling. Fortunately for Kenneth's finances, there was no horseracing to bet on in south-eastern Italy in the early autumn of 1944.

Having obtained the good sherry, we were determined to find some glasses more suitable to drink it out of than the thick tumblers improvised from beer bottles that were in general use. We drove our jeep to the small hilltop town of Cerignola and found just what we wanted there, a shop selling glass and chinaware. While Kenneth went inside to buy sherry glasses I remained outside to guard the jeep. While sitting there I became aware of a curious figure approaching down the street. It was a woman, wearing a huge picture hat against the strong noonday sun, her more than ample form concealed in the folds of a flowing pink cotton dress. As she reached the back of the jeep I could see that her cheeks were thickly rouged and her lips scarlet with make-up. 'Good morning,' she said in English and then, losing no time in introducing her subject of choice, quickly added, 'Have you got cigarettes?' I had been joined by Kenneth with the sherry glasses. We told her 'No', but sensing that there might be something worth pursuing, added that we could probably bring some tomorrow. 'Good,' she said. 'You must come to lunch with me. I live there,' and she pointed to a large iron-studded wooden door 100 yards down the street.

Neither Kenneth nor I smoked, so we had no trouble collecting 200 cigarettes from our NAAFI ration and we drove with them to Cerignola the next day. In response to our ring the iron-studded door was opened and we drove into a cavernous stone-flagged hall with a roof supported by sturdy stone pillars. A flight of stone steps led up into the house which was wholly contained within the town walls. In the house we were in a different world. It was luxuriously furnished, the floors were thickly carpeted, and the walls draped with tapestries. One small room was occupied by a beautiful boy in his late teens who was introduced to us as a geography student. It was largely filled by an enormous four-poster bed which left just enough room for an upright chair and table covered with geography text books and an atlas. There was a connecting door to her bedroom.

Lunch was served by a manservant in a white jacket and gloves. The main course was a rich chicken casserole, followed by peaches and nectarines and a hard local cheese and bread. The wine was rough and grainy and made from grapes grown in the vineyard which began on the slopes immediately below the house windows and extended down into the plain. The geography student sat quietly and demurely, not speaking a word, throughout lunch. It soon emerged that our hostess had other demands besides cigarettes. She wanted tyres. Her car was immobilized because the tyres were worn out and she could not get any new ones. It was disgraceful, she said, but she was sure we could help. We told her firmly: cigarettes *yes*, tyres *no*. It must have been very frustrating for her. When she had to accept that no tyres would be forthcoming we ceased to be quite such welcome guests. Tyres or no tyres, she probably survived the rest of the war reasonably well fed and in reasonable comfort with her geography student.

After we had spent a fortnight guarding dummy tanks the strategic plan was changed. Instead of being on the axis of the Florence to Bologna road through the central Apennines, the main Eighth Army thrust against the Gothic Line was to be on the narrow coastal plain beside the Adriatic – where the dummy tanks had been intended to mislead the enemy to expect it. Although the plain was broken by numerous spurs and rivers flowing down from the mountains, it certainly provided more scope for the deployment of tanks than the central mountain route. Perhaps the Germans interpreted the dummy tanks as a subtle double bluff. In any case Kenneth and I were redundant in our dummy tanks role, and we returned to our regiments.

In the next few weeks we moved by stages up the Adriatic coast, gradually getting closer to the Gothic Line, the last important defensive line stretching from the area of Rimini, a port and beach resort on the Adriatic coast, along the spine of the Apennines to the Mediterranean at La Spezia. At one stopping place we set up the A Squadron Mess in a substantial stone-built house surrounded by a belt of oaks and chestnuts. At the back it had a rose garden ringed by a semi-circular stone balustrade which gave the impression of an orderly country life style. The lady of the house, a middle-aged widow, kept her own apartments while we occupied the rest of the house. After supper in the mess I went in to see her, knocking at her sitting-room door and receiving a softly spoken invitation to come in. I found her seated on a sofa, with a small table in front of her on which stood an oil lamp, the only illumination in the room, and the threads for the crochet work she was doing were spread on her knees. The lamp gave a small pool of light, with the rest of the room in shadow and substantial pieces of furniture and family portraits on the walls dimly visible in the gloom.

She waved me to a chair and I sat down. She was wearing a dark red jumper and a grey skirt, while her black hair, flecked with grey, fell to her shoulders, framing a pale oval face. She was strikingly beautiful. Her English was almost perfect and, after a few minutes of general conversation, she changed to the topic that really concerned her – the welfare of her estate workers. They were very short of food – on the verge of starvation, she said. She begged me to get a supply of food for them. I explained that food rations were issued to an army unit on the basis of the number of men in that unit, and those numbers were inelastic; we had no authority to feed the civilian population, and if we made an exception in one case we would be embarking on a slippery slope. We could not do it. She had laid her crochet work aside on the sofa, leaving her delicate hands free to emphasize her argument. She was reluctant to accept that my response was final. It was not merely her male workers that were involved, she said. They had families, wives and children. Surely I did not want the children to go hungry. I suspected that she, too, was short of food, but was far too proud to say so. It took me fully half an hour to convince her that I could not help. Her sincerity, her concern for her workers, her animation, the sweet tones of her slightly accented voice, made it painful to deny her. I had been deprived of female company for many months; nor for many months had any woman so appealed to my senses, and I would have found it easy to fall in love with her. How wonderful it would have been to tell her that some magic cornucopia had opened, showering blessings and supplies of food, that her worries were over. Instead I had to say goodbye and leave her alone in that dark room.

Outside in the passage I stopped and leant back against the wall. I felt a profound sadness that war inflicted, quite apart from the destruction, cruelty and loss of life, so much pain on the innocent and the beautiful. Presently I wiped the back of my hand across my eyes, stood up and went to join my comrades of A Squadron.

The next day we resumed our march to the north. I did not even know her name, and of course I never saw her again. But I had lasting memories of that tree-girt garden in the dusk, with unpruned rose bushes stirring in a gentle evening breeze, and of that lovely woman, so calm and yet so passionate, in the fitful light of an oil lamp.

Chapter Ten

Coriano and Montecieco

During the month of August, through a process of order, counter-order and disorder as we adjusted to the ever-changing requirements of the strategic plan, we made our way by stages up the Adriatic coast. One evening at the end of the month we were encamped on a wooded hill overlooking the sea. I was standing at the edge of the wood, with a view of the beach, the sea, and the local fishing fleet coming in. In the foreground the unruffled sea was pale blue, receding into a misty grey blur at the horizon. At first sight the fishing boats were tiny white triangles in the mist. Then, as they approached, the brown and red hulls of the half dozen boats took shape beneath the sails; finally the heads and shoulders of the fishermen became visible above the gunwales. As the prows hit the beach, crew members vaulted out into the shallow water and hauled the boats up onto the sand, and began immediately to unload their catch. As I contemplated this peaceful scene, I became aware of a footfall behind me, and turned to see Sergeant Taylor, with his characteristic high-stepping gait, coming through the undergrowth. We greeted each other, and he said, 'May I have a word, sir?' I said of course, and then he said, 'I have to tell you sir, that the tank crews would not be happy to go into action under Major Dance.' It was totally unexpected and utterly shattering. Extreme thoughts raced through my head. Was this mutiny, this expression of unwillingness to go into action under a lawfully appointed commander? And if so, how should I react? But within seconds I realized that the idea of mutiny was absurd. Ginger Taylor was an old regular soldier of the highest quality, the senior troop sergeant in the squadron, immensely efficient, a charming companion, loyal and, above all, extremely brave. It was unthinkable that he would take the action he had unless he was motivated by the strongest convictions, backed by a consensus of the tank crews.

Moreover, I knew that he was right. Jimmy had taken over command of the squadron when Jackie had gone home in February and, during the intervening months, there had been frequent evidence of his incompetence and preference for pleasure over duty. Things had come to a head two nights earlier when, on coming from a regimental order group, he had tried to pass on the orders for the next phase of the advance to the squadron tank commanders. We gathered in a semi-circle in the darkness, and Jimmy had stammered in tongue-tied incoherence and completely failed to deliver his message. It was a staggering exposure of inadequacy in an officer. After Taylor had spoken I was overcome by a feeling of shame that I had done nothing, indeed had laughed to myself in the darkness when I should have been appalled. I needed time to think, time to find a way out of this dilemma. So I temporized, telling Taylor that I understood, but that he must give me a little time to consider the next step, the best and right thing to do. He accepted this and went back to his tank. The vital question to be answered was this: if regicide were to be achieved and Jimmy was to be deposed, who would succeed him, with only a day or two or so before we would be in action? The proper first successor was Tom Toller, the nominal second-in-command of the squadron, but Tom could not be considered as a possible leader of men and tanks into battle. He was the most likeable of men, but he was handicapped by an incurable addiction to falling in love. Wherever we were, and however unpromising the circumstances, Tom would find some female to whom he would lose his heart. His eyes became glazed, and nothing interested him, nothing registered with him, except planning and arranging his next tryst with his loved one. As soon as we moved the spell was broken. His vision cleared and for some days he took an interest in whatever was going on and could talk on a variety of subjects. Then you noticed one morning that his eyes were glazed; Tom was in love again. The men were fond of him because of his complete lack of pomposity and affectation. They would follow him anywhere, but he would not have the faintest idea which way to go. Ginger Taylor knew him well, and it was significant that he had come to me, the squadron's second captain.

I was still agonizing over the problem when I received the news that Jackie had arrived back at the regiment after being an instructor at Sandhurst and a squadron leader in the 24th Lancers during the first weeks of the Normandy campaign. Immensely relieved, I hurried to regimental headquarters where I found him and explained what had happened. He grasped the situation immediately and went to see the Commanding Officer, Daniel Asquith. Within an hour everything was settled. Jackie was reinstated as commander of A Squadron and Jimmy, who had been suffering from a minor intestinal trouble, was on his way to Rome with orders not to return to the regiment until he was fully restored to health. We never saw him again before the end of the war. A heavy weight was lifted from my shoulders.

Jackie had the confidence of everyone. He had the right pedigree, as he was the only son of Lieutenant General Sir Wentworth (Jakes) Harman KCB DSO, the Colonel of the Regiment during the Second World War. Jackie had inherited the same instinctive 'feel' for the army that Johnny Tatham-Warter had possessed, and among Bays' officers they were the two supreme professionals. I was lucky to be commanded by them in battle. However, his character had certain anomalies. He was the fastest runner of his day at Wellington College, and as a wing three-quarter on the rugger field he should have been able to outpace his opposite numbers and score tries. But if anyone threatened to tackle him he would pull up instead of going flat out for the try line; he was regarded as a funk. His rugger persona did not seem a good augury for performance in war, yet surprisingly on the battlefield he never shirked danger and was as brave as anyone.

There was a cruel streak, the hint of a bully, in his nature. He constantly nagged Chris Parker, one of the A Squadron officers. 'You are nothing but a bloody little girl,' he would shout at Chris in the Mess. Chris was small, dark, quiet and a little effeminate in manner. He was also intelligent, hardworking, an officer who devoted himself to the interests of his men and was loved and respected by them, and had been awarded the MC for gallantry in command of the regimental reconnaissance troop at Second Alamein. There was no conceivable justification for Jackie's taunts. Jackie tended to find the misfortunes of others a source of amusement. In his autobiography, *Gone for a Soldier*, John Stanier recounted how, when he was commanding the Scots Greys in 1970, Jackie, the divisional commander, ordered him to wade a river to see whether it was a suitable crossing for tanks on a forthcoming exercise. Stanier wrote:

> I stepped gingerly into the freezing water. I got half way across when I stepped into a great hole about twelve feet deep and was swept away downstream by the current. I managed to swim to the bank and dragged myself out spluttering and shaking to find Jackie and his staff killing themselves with laughter by the river.

Whether the staff officers found John's predicament as funny as Jackie did or not, no doubt they thought it diplomatic to laugh if the General laughed. Some show of concern and a helping hand would have been more appropriate.

Discussing his future late in the war in Italy, Douglas MacCallan and I agreed that Jackie was sure to become a general, but we believed that major general and command of a division was his ceiling. He was a practical, not an intellectual soldier, and academic gifts greater than his were needed, we thought, to attain the very highest rank. Consequently he exceeded our expectations when he became a full general, Adjutant-General to the Forces and Deputy Supreme Allied Commander Europe. All the same Sir John Stanier, an outstandingly intellectual officer, ultimately outranked him, becoming one of the last of the field marshals.

Jackie had taken over A Squadron just in time. Two days later we were on the march northwards on appalling rutted tracks, blinded and choked by clouds of dust churned up by the tank tracks. We were being urged to make all the haste we could. The Eighth Army assault on the Gothic Line had begun on 27 August and quickly broke through the

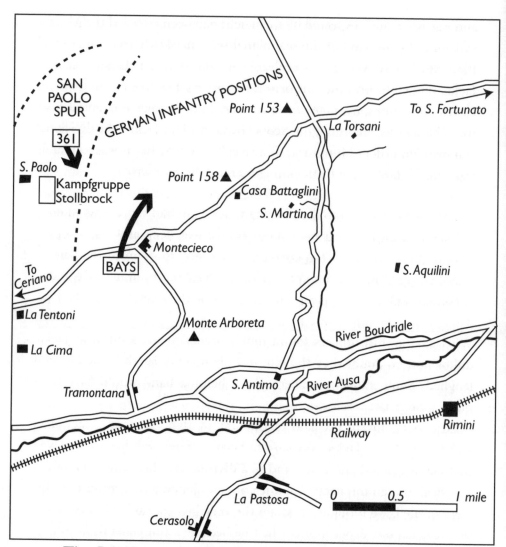

SAN
PAOLO
SPUR

GERMAN INFANTRY POSITIONS

Point 153 ▲

To S. Fortunato

La Torsani

361

S. Paolo

Kampfgruppe
Stollbrock

Point 158 ▲

Casa Battaglini

S. Martina

S. Aquilini

Montecieco

To
Ceriano

BAYS

La Tentoni

Monte Arboreta

River Boudriale

La Cima

Tramontana

S. Antimo

River Ausa

Railway

Rimini

La Pastosa

0   0.5   1 mile

Cerasolo

The BAYS attack on Point 153, 20 September 1944

Map 5: The Gothic Line – Point 153 and Montecieco.

outer crust of the Line on the River Foglia whose mouth was at the town of Pesaro. Optimism stirred in the breasts of the Higher Command: of Field Marshal Alexander, Commander in Chief Allied Armies in Italy; of General Sir Oliver Leese, commander of the Eighth Army: and General Charles Keightley, commander of V Corps. They believed that they had the Germans on the run, and that it was just a matter of harrying them and pursuing them all the way to the valley of the Po, across northern Italy, through the Ljubljana Gap and on to Vienna. Such optimism was misplaced. The position on the Foglia was indeed the strongest part of the Gothic Line, but in fact the description 'Line' was a misnomer; rather was it a series of defended localities twenty miles deep, admittedly in varying stages of preparedness, stretching all the way back from Pesaro to the bigger port and beach resort of Rimini; and once it became apparent to Kesselring, the German commander-in-chief, that the main Allied offensive effort was being made in the narrow gap between the Apennines and the Adriatic he was able to reinforce it with formations drawn from other parts of the front.

After a series of exhausting forced marches in the most trying conditions, the Bays caught up with the action on the river Conca on 4 September, the ninth day of the battle. The Conca, with a road running beside it, followed a somewhat tortuous course. It flowed down from the mountains into the plain, took a right-angle bend to the right to flow straight for a couple of miles and then turned left to reach the sea at Cattolica. We crossed the lower reaches of the river. The Germans, we were told, were in disorderly retreat, and our orders were to go straight in, without pause for rest or tank maintenance, and complete the rout. The forward troops of 46th Infantry Division were reported to be on the ridge ahead, and that was to be our start line. Maximum speed was essential. There was no time to disseminate information to tank commanders. Squadron leaders, who had been briefed by the colonel, should lead their squadrons up to the start line.

These reports were a mass of misinformation. 46th Division patrols, if they had ever reached the Coriano ridge – it was probably a case of faulty map-reading – had been pushed back off it; and the Germans, far from being on the verge of rout, were occupying prepared positions on the ridge in strength. The regiment began the advance to the start line two squadrons up, C Squadron left on the road beside the river and A Squadron right on slightly higher ground. After covering about half the distance C Squadron, commanded by Major 'Washy' Hibbert, came under heavy anti-tank fire from the hill top village of San Gemmano on the south side of the river which dominated that part of the valley. With the river on one side and a deep ditch on the other the squadron could not take up effective fire positions to reply, and when one of their tanks was knocked out blocking the way back the way they had come they had no option but to continue towards the start line. Their subsequent adventures were the subject of a report by the squadron second in command, John McVail, immediately afterwards:

As we moved forward we machine gunned everything – hedges, ditches, houses, haystacks, in fact every possible place which might conceal the enemy, and when we came to a village we put HE into the corner houses while our scatter gunners machine gunned the doors and lower windows of the houses, the commander at the same time tommy gunning the top windows. These tactics at first proved successful and the noise and confusion must have frightened the enemy as several of them ran out of their ditches and fox holes and tried to run for it, but many of them were caught in our fire.

Just south of S. Savino (a small village on the ridge) we had our first real piece of excitement when a bazooka man leapt out of a ditch behind Major Hibbert's tank and tried to knock him out. Major Hibbert shot him with his pistol. North of S. Savino we passed by a few feet a Mark IV tank with its 75mm gun trained on the road. We passed so quickly that not one of us fired a shot. We then realized that we were cut off and in a desperate position, and every time we halted to try and make a plan we were fired on from every conceivable angle and had to move on. Also in the back of our minds we could visualize the Mark IV creeping out from its position and striking us from the rear. Eventually we reached K.13 (a marker stone 3 kilometres short of Coriano) at S. Maria and when Captain McVail's tank went round the corner and the dust cleared he was confronted by a Mark IV tank reversing as fast as it could go down the road. The two tanks halted with guns pointed at each other at a range of 15 yards. Captain McVail's tank opened fire with an HE which was already loaded in his gun. Troopers Corbett and Jumps, the loader and gunner, then got off four more shots before the German could reply. The Mark IV brewed up and one man baled out. He tried to make a bolt for it but was machine gunned and killed before he could get back to his friends. At this moment Major Hibbert's tank was hit and immobilized and the crew baled out. The road was now blocked in both directions. Captain McVail's tank pulled over to the left of the road to a house behind which Major Hibbert and his crew were hiding, and a conference was held.

Fire was still coming from all directions and it was only a question of time before the other tank was hit. We ran for cover just as our own artillery opened fire and our tank received a direct hit and caught fire. We lay low until somebody spotted a dug-out and one by one we ran for it.

The dug-out was a large one and had been made with care. It was propped, had supports in the ceiling and was situated in the side of a steep bank. It contained a chair, a pillow, a sieve, a half-empty bottle of Chianti and four empty ones, a basket and a quantity of straw. We held a conference and decided to stay for the night in the hopes that our troops would capture the village either that night of the following morning.

Those hopes were disappointed, and after forty-eight hours the C Squadron party, having collected five German prisoners in the meantime, made their way back by night to the British lines.

When C Squadron came under fire from San Gemmano, A Squadron was ordered to turn left and support them. It was an ill-fated manoeuvre. We were crossing a field of deep plough in which several tanks in turning lost their tracks and we were no help to C Squadron. When we turned back to continue our own advance more tracks were lost and we came under concentrated artillery and anti-tank fire from the ridge, making further progress impossible. So our first day in the Italian campaign came to a thoroughly frustrating end.

The Coriano ridge was not captured until a week later, and it took the equivalent of three and a half infantry divisions to do it. San Savino, the village that C Squadron had passed on the first day of the battle, was taken by two battalions of Gurkhas with the support of B and C Squadrons of the Bays as protection against counter-attack. A Squadron was in reserve and so had no direct part in the battle. The ridge which had been designated as the start line for a push against a disintegrating enemy was held by three crack and battle-hardened German divisions – the 26th Panzer, the 29th Panzer Grenadier and the 1st Parachute. Faulty intelligence could hardly have been more complete.

The next week was spent in pursuit of the Germans across broken country until the ten-mile gap between Rimini and the tiny mountain republic of San Marino (population 25,000) was reached. There the river Ausa flowed at the foot of slopes that rose to the Fortunato feature just outside Rimini. The feature was extended by the San Martino in Venti ridge which was the last defensible position before the multi-channelled river Marécchia and the plain of Lombardy and rose at its south-westerly end, through the village of Ceriano, to the heights of San Marino. On 18 September the Bays had closed up to the river Ausa, but were caught there in impenetrable congestion. The only available bridge at Rovereta had been destroyed by the Germans, and the alternative crossing, the ford at Benefizio, could not cope with the volume of traffic going forward. From that time until the end of the battle I was fraught with a persistent feeling of claustrophobia as the traffic of several divisions competed for space on narrow roads and tracks lined with deep ditches into which tanks could slide irretrievably, and intermittent shelling added to the general confusion. While the rest of the regiment was held up south of the Ausa, A Squadron was ordered forward to support the Yorkshire Dragoons, the motor battalion of 2 Armoured Brigade, in their attack on Monte Arboreta, an isolated hill a mile short of the San Martino in Venti ridge and commanding the road from the Ausa to the ridge. The Yorkshire Dragoons were engaged in a fierce battle, taking Monte Arboreta, being forced off it by a German counter-attack and finally retaking it, albeit with heavy casualties. A Squadron suffered no casualties, but fired off most of their ammunition and used up most of their petrol in manoeuvring round the hill. Owing to continuing congestion at the Benefizio ford the supply trucks were unable to get up to replenish our petrol and ammunition, a fact which was to be our salvation in the dire happenings of 20 September.

The Bays finally got clear of the congestion at the ford on the afternoon of 19 September and began to make their way up the road to Montecieco, with its cluster of houses including a school, on the San Martino in Venti ridge. The V Corps' plan prescribed an attack by the Bays on Point 153 that evening, but the delay at the ford had been so protracted that Daniel Asquith, the commanding officer, decided that it was too late and postponed the attack till the next morning. The regiment went into leaguer on the west side of the road and were rejoined there by A Squadron. On the morning of 20 September events unfolded rapidly. The regiment moved out of leaguer before first light and advanced to a position a hundred yards west of the road junction at Montecieco, where they were hull-down on the rim of a huge tilted grassy bowl whose top edge was at Ceriano and the buildings at Casa Cima and Casa Tentoni. As dawn broke I could see three or four Churchill tanks dotted about the bowl. Their turrets were closed and there was no sign of life around them. I assumed that they were either knocked out or broken down, but that afternoon they suddenly started up and moved away down the valley towards the Ausa, their presence and purpose unexplained. Point 153, which the regiment was to attack, was a mile to the north-east of Montecieco, commanding a crossroads on the ridge and the lower ground of the San Fortunato feature further north–east which the Canadians were attacking. While the regiment was forming up it was harassed by sniper fire from a house near Montecieco and small-arms and anti-tank fire from the rear in the area of Ceriano. Asquith decided that it was impossible to attack until the threat from the rear was eliminated and ordered B Squadron to send a troop to deal with it. Two tanks from that troop were quickly knocked out and Sergeant Burley's tank continued alone. In and out of his tank for fully half an hour, Don Burley fought the most gallant of actions against superior numbers of German infantry until he was wounded by a grenade, when he returned to his tank and rejoined B Squadron in time to take part in the attack on Point 153.

At 9.50 orders were received that the attack on Point 153 was to go in at 10.15. Asquith objected in vain that the high ground to his rear was still held by the enemy, that the route to the objective was covered by anti-tank guns to the north and several tanks had been knocked out already, and that his reserve squadron was nearly out of petrol and ammunition. The Brigadier, Richard Goodbody, answered that all that was well-known, but the attack was a vital part of the Corps' plan to relieve pressure on the Canadians and must go in as scheduled. So this suicidal attack by B and C Squadron was duly launched. The moment they left their hull-down positions in the bowl they were exposed to a storm of fire from the 75mm self-propelled guns and the 88mm anti-tank guns of *Kampfgruppe* Stollbrock in the hamlets of San Paolo and Piano dei Venti on the spur running down from the vicinity of Ceriano to the Marécchia valley. The area is almost treeless and fields of fire were uninterrupted. The range was about 600 yards, tantamount to point blank for accurate German anti-tank guns, and the tanks of the two squadrons were picked off one after another without a hope of reply. Captain Chrisophel of the self-propelled gun company of the 361st Regiment wrote of Lieutenant Rossler:

As soon as he saw 27 Shermans advancing, he took the initiative and decided to go forward as far as possible and with his three self-propelled guns and put 13 tanks out of action in a very short time.

Spurred on by his example, the grenadiers were sucked into action and destroyed a further 9 Shermans.

Under cover of smoke three tanks from B Squadron got back safely behind the start line, none from C. Any possibility of an effective response from our supporting artillery, the Honourable Artillery Company (HAC), was undone when the tank of our FOO, Quentin Drage, was knocked out and he was killed while accompanying the leading elements of C Squadron.

At that time I was the A Squadron rear link, which meant that my radio was on the same frequency as the rear links of the other squadrons and the commanding officer, and I was the intermediary between the commanding officer and my squadron leader, Jackie Harman, whose set was on the same frequency as the rest of the tanks in the squadron. Obviously Asquith was under pressure to renew the attack using A Squadron, because he called me up and said, 'Have you got enough petrol for a few miles?' I answered with an uncompromising 'No'. He then said, 'Not enough for one little canter?' Again I said 'No' and that was the end of the matter. I think I saved the squadron from one suicidal mission. It was then about midday. Shortly afterwards a squadron of the 9th Lancers under Derek Alhusen was sent up to come under the command of the Bays for another assault on Point 153. Their colonel, Jack Price, came with them and, after conferring with Daniel Asquith, spoke to the brigadier saying that the 9th Lancers were ready to attack and every crewman was ready to carry out his duty as a soldier, but the British were going to lose another armoured regiment if a different plan of attack was not adopted. Brigadier Goodbody took responsibility for cancelling the attack and ordering Price merely to consolidate their position. After the battle he was relieved of his command.

The original plan of V Corps' commander, Charles Keightley, had two fundamental flaws. Firstly, the objective was not visible from the start line because Point 158 with the farmhouse Casa Battaglini intervened. Secondly, it involved movement across the front of a strongly-held enemy position and exposure to short-range fire from anti-tank guns in the rear and left rear – a manoeuvre that could not possibly succeed. It was clear that the proper route for an attack on Point 153 was northward from Monte Arboreta to hit the San Martino in Venti ridge north-east of Point 158 and then along the ridge road to the Point 153 crossroads. Indeed that was the plan successfully adopted the same evening, which led to the Germans abandoning all their positions south of the River Marécchia during the night. The Bays' attack that morning had been both needlessly costly and utterly futile.

Don Burley's tank was knocked out and he was again wounded in B Squadron's abortive attack, but he survived after taking refuge in a fold in the ground while the firing was intense. His actions that day were the finest and bravest of any member of The Queen's Bays in the Second World War, and he was awarded the DCM. The citation concluded, 'This NCO, throughout, showed resource, initiative, powers of planning and skill in execution which would be considered outstanding in a commander of much higher rank.' He recovered quickly from his wounds and took part in the river line battles that followed later in the autumn of 1944. He left the Army in 1946 and had a successful career in business, living to the great age of 94 before he died in February 2013.

In 1946 later a memorial was erected and dedicated at the exact spot from which the attack was launched to honour those members of the regiment who had died in the battles of Coriano and Montecieco. It was a simple white stone plaque set in a brick frame and surrounded by a balustrade supported by brick pillars. A flight of steps gave access to it from the road. The plaque was engraved with the names of the fallen – names which included those of Jackie Harman's 'bloody little girl' and Military Cross holder Chris Parker and John McVail, a survivor and chronicler of C Squadron's astonishing exploit at Coriano. It may be the only memorial to an armoured regiment in Italy.

The total of sixty-four casualties in the space of a few minutes made 20 September 1944 the worst day of the war for the Queen's Bays. Douglas MacCallan's tank was one of the first knocked out that morning and, although unwounded, he, like Don Burley, spent several hours sheltering in a fold of the ground while shells and bullets flew continuously around and above him, before he was able to crawl back over the ridge. So his comment in a letter to his father written a week later stands out as a masterpiece of understatement, 'Life here is a bit "choppy". I lost a bit of kit again the other day.'

In late September 1994, exactly half a century after the tragic day at Montecieco, I visited the Gothic Line battlefields in company with Jackie Harman and Douglas MacCallan. We established ourselves in the somewhat faded Edwardian red plush splendour of the Grand Hotel in Rimini. It was out of season and the hotel was almost empty, its atmosphere deserted and depressing. Nearby is a wide sandy beach, no doubt teeming with holidaymakers in the summer months. The temperature was still summerlike, and we were blessed with real 'shirtsleeve' weather. Our first visit was to the CWGC War Cemetery at Coriano, where several of our colleagues are buried. Like all cemeteries cared for by the Commonwealth War Graves Commission it was immaculately kept, with masses of red roses. From there we drove in a hired car the few miles to the isolated church in a grove of holm oaks at San Clemente which was the start point for A Squadron's advance towards the Coriano ridge on 4 September 1944. We walked out onto the same ploughed field where so many tanks lost their tracks in 1944, and found the going tough and obviously cloying for tank tracks. Next we descended the hill to the Conca valley and took the road along the river bank to San Savino, but could find no sign of the dug-out that had been a refuge for C Squadron in 1944. No doubt it had been filled in and the props used for firewood years before.

The following two days were spent in exploration of the Montecieco area. For this part of the trip we were joined by the Italian military historian Amedeo Montemaggi. He was tall, slim with grey hair and moustache, and his character too was somewhat grey. My two companions found him a bore. He was a specialist in the battles of the Gothic Line, and fifty years after these battles was still producing books and pamphlets, in Italian and English, on his subject. Like all specialists, he had a one-track mind. However, I found him interesting because his researches had given him an intimate knowledge of the fighting from the German viewpoint. Without his contribution we should never have known where the 75s and 88s were placed on the San Paulo spur, or how the stalwart *Kampfgruppe* Stollbrock had held up the British advance all day on 20 September. Knowing the position of the anti-tank guns brought home to us how hopelessly misconceived was the order to attack Point 153 from Montecieco.

We drove to Point 153, which of course we never reached in 1944. It is occupied by a pleasant farmhouse surrounded by trees and a mature garden, with extensive views of rolling, almost downs-like countryside, and vineyards in the valleys. It is no more than five miles from the middle of Rimini, but seems much more remote. If the attack had ever got that far, our tanks would have had a steep climb to the point and would have been very vulnerable to the defenders. We found the memorial in pristine condition – no weeds and the stone surface free of moss and algae. This was thanks to the regular attention of the children of Montecieco School, so we visited the school to thank the children and the charming schoolmistress, and to make a contribution to the school's finances. An ugly concrete cube of unknown purpose had been built close to the memorial. We discovered that it belonged to the Rimini water company, and Montemaggi agreed to convey our complaint about its presence to the company, who responded by planting a hedge to hide it. The Commonwealth War Graves Commission had recently taken responsibility for the upkeep of the memorial.

Chapter Eleven

The End in Italy

On the evening of 20 September 1944 A Squadron, having spent most of the day sheltering hull-down in the grassy bowl, was back in the Ausa valley in leaguer with the rest of the regiment. There we learnt that the higher command, tacitly admitting that Italy, with its mountainous terrain and hundreds of fast-flowing rivers, offered no scope for the tactical employment of armoured divisions as such, had decided to disband 1st Armoured Division. However, 2 Armoured Brigade, composed of The Queen's Bays, 9th Lancers and 10th Hussars, with a rifle battalion and the 11th (HAC) RHA, would remain as an independent formation with its sole function co-operation with infantry.

John Combe was appointed to command the brigade. He had commanded 11th Hussars, known as the Cherry Pickers, an extremely successful armoured car regiment, in the desert, and was a very sound soldier. He was a rich man, and owned and bred some high class racehorses after the war, winning the 1000 Guineas with Big Berry. But he was not a big spender; in the field he always wore army issue boots, and his mackintosh was always an army issue gas cape. His gas cape had plenty of use in the autumn of 1944. There had been an autumnal chill in the air in the days before Montecieco, and the weather broke that evening and gave us a thorough drenching. Heavy rains continued intermittently for the next three months, making it what the local inhabitants described as the wettest autumn in living memory.

Second Armoured Brigade was placed under the command of 46th Infantry Division. The plan of campaign for the rest of the year was an advance up the line of the Via Emilia, the highway that runs as straight as an arrow up the north-east side of the Apennines from Rimini to Bologna, the city on which the American Fifth Army was converging through the mountains North of Florence. The 46th Division's line led through the foothills, which comprised steep-sided spurs separated every few miles by rivers swollen into torrents by the incessant rains. Often the rivers overflowed, flooding the surrounding fields and making them impassable to tanks. As tank country it was far from ideal.

The regular tactical procedure at each river line was for the infantry to make a night attack and form a bridgehead, and then for an armoured regiment or squadron to cross as soon as a bridge was installed to protect the infantry against the inevitable counter-attack. After one of these manoeuvres A Squadron had taken up a defensive position on a bare hillside, with a farm surrounded by a dense cactus hedge a hundred yards to the left of my tank. There was a lull, one of those inexplicable pauses when no gun fires and silence falls on the battlefield. Suddenly a terrible squawking started up behind the cactus hedge, and moments later a chicken, flying for its life, burst through the hedge pursued by a Gurkha wielding his kukri. The pursuit continued for only a few yards in the open before one swish of the kukri removed the chicken's head cleanly. The Gurkha bent down, picked up the decapitated chicken, tucked it under his arm and disappeared back through the hedge. Soon the guns began to fire again and battle recommenced. One of the rivers was the Rubicone, a river name famous from the history of Julius Caesar and preserved in the terminology of the card game Piquet (pronounced Pick-ette), but unexceptional as Apennine rivers go. It flows out of the mountains past the small town of Savignano and empties into the Adriatic twenty miles north-west of Rimini.

A Squadron was constantly in and out of the line, and, as second-in-command, I was always in close proximity to the squadron leader, Jackie Harman, in my Sherman equipped with the latest gun, the 76mm. As the going across country was often waterlogged, we were liable to be confined to the few roads and tracks and farmyards which became congested with the vehicles of several different formations. One day we were in a small farmyard with three carriers of the Leicesters. The platoon sergeant was sitting on the back of one of the carriers with his right leg over the side when one of the other carriers, trying to turn, came too close and sliced his calf cleanly from his leg. There was no blood, but the flesh was dry and grey. He must have been in agony, but he insisted on taking time to hand over the platoon roll to his corporal before he would allow himself to be carried to an ambulance. He was a very brave professional soldier.

Divisional intelligence summaries were circulated regularly. Besides giving the latest reports of enemy movements, losses and casualties, they sometimes included excerpts from letters taken from PoWs. Some of these painted an unflattering picture of the German soldier as a domesticated animal. One letter home written by an infantryman and taken from him before he was able to post it stated, 'When we left the house to retreat we did not forget to leave our brown visiting card in the cupboard.'

A Squadron's last battle of 1944, and the last battle of Eighth Army's autumn campaign, was at the River Lamone which flowed through the eastern outskirts of the town of Faenza. By then we were forty miles beyond Rimini and had left the considerable towns of Cesena and Forli on the Via Emilia behind. Hills rose abruptly on the left, the far bank of the Lamone, to a height of 1,200 feet, and made it the strongest defended position we had faced since Montecieco. The Lincolns of 138 Brigade were one of the units that had reached the top, and had then switched right to face the lower ground towards Faenza, supported by the four troops of A Squadron. Jackie Harman and I in our two headquarters tanks had managed to climb a steep narrow track through a thick wood to a ledge just below the crest, where we took up position behind a two-storey house which turned out to be the country residence of a Faenza dentist. Fortunately he and his family were away, presumably at a house in the town. A solid projectile had broken through the wall at the top of the stairs, leaving a jagged hole, and left through another jagged hole in the wall above the front door, missing by inches a glass-fronted cabinet on the landing which contained his collection of china figures. The house was well and comfortably furnished, but the dentist was left with a substantial bill for repairs.

The attack across the Lamone had begun on the evening of 3 December and continued indecisively for the next four days as the Lincolns tried to advance on the road junction of Celle two miles outside Faenza, supported by the A Squadron troops of Lieutenants Levett and Munro. Those troops were totally isolated. Heavy night rains had made movement off the roads impossible, and movement on the roads and tracks was difficult owing to mines and craters. Existence in the tanks at night was fraught with tension as German patrols, like the biblical hosts of Midian, prowled around. Bazooka men tried to stalk the tanks, and one of them was shot dead only six yards from Colin Munro's tank. The crews had to sleep in very cramped conditions inside the tanks, taking it in turns to keep watch.

The Germans brought up 508th Heavy Tank Battalion and the 90th Panzer Grenadier Division to reinforce the defences of Faenza and counter-attack. The tank battalion included some Tigers, giant steel fortresses on tracks; and the Panzer Grenadiers were the successors of the old 90th Light Division of *Afrikakorps* fame, which had been partially destroyed and reformed several times, and renamed. At dawn on 8 December a heavy artillery barrage fell on the leading 46th Division positions, followed by an infantry attack. One of the forward companies of the Lincolns was quickly overrun, and the tanks of Colin Munro's troop were knocked out after putting up strenuous resistance. At squadron headquarters we hastened to pack up, start our tanks and prepare to move out and take a defensive position on the ridge at the back of the dentist's house. Meanwhile panic had set in at the nearby headquarters of the Lincolns. As Jackie and I were climbing into our tanks Colonel Bell, the commanding officer of the Lincolns, appeared on the ground beside us, convinced that we were about to leave him in the lurch. 'You're abandoning us,' he cried out in tones in which fear and reproach were mixed in roughly equal proportions. We assured him that our intentions were the precise opposite. Minutes later we were in position, facing a wide expanse of open ground with a belt of trees on either side. If the Germans had tried to advance across the open ground we should have had an ideal shoot, but if they had come through the trees we should have been in greater trouble. Neither eventuality arose. The defensive fire of our own artillery soon silenced the German batteries, and caused their infantry heavy casualties. By the afternoon the attack had petered out. A renewal of the attack was expected the next day, but the Germans had had enough and it never came. In the course of the fighting that day, Captain John Brunt, a Sherwood Forester attached to 6th Lincolns, earned the Victoria Cross for his determined leadership of the defence of a position. Attacking the enemy with a Bren gun, he accounted for fourteen dead Germans before he ran out of ammunition. Switching to using a PIAT and then a 2-inch mortar his aggressive stance played a major part in repelling the German attack. Brunt never knew that he had earned the VC as he was killed while having his breakfast the next morning.

After the defeat of the counter-attack the infantry of 46th Division, who had been continuously in action for six days, were relieved by the New Zealanders. Our A Squadron tank crews were relieved by crews from C Squadron, who came up to take over the seventeen tanks involved in position, as the movement of fresh tanks was impossible in sodden conditions. From our position on the ridge the squadron headquarters crews trudged on foot down a steep muddy path in the dark to the river valley, where we were met by carriers and transported over the Lamone Bailey bridge at first light to our waiting regimental trucks on the east side. That night had brought the first frost of the winter, and in the open carriers without overcoats, it had been a bitterly cold ride. From there we were taken to the regiment's winter quarters in comfortable houses near Pesaro, where the Gothic Line campaign had been launched three months beforehand.

Colin Munro escaped unhurt, as did his crew, when his tank was knocked out. As a postscript to the battle, he was awarded the MC for gallantry at the Lamone.

The winter of 1944-45 was a cold one in northern Italy. We kept cheerful with gin from a factory in Bari and a truly delectable, smooth vermouth from a factory in Forlí. For weeks on end the roads were bound by frost and easily motorable. When the thaw came in early February the sheer volume of military traffic broke through the surface crust of roads already weakened by shellfire and reduced them to treacherous bogs in which trucks foundered and stuck. Such were the road conditions that some change-overs had to be cancelled as vehicles, including tanks, bogged down or were unable to move. It was not until the warmth of an early spring made road mending possible that the roads dried out and travelling got back to normal.

We did not spend the whole winter in the comfort of our billets at Pesaro. In the middle of January we were sent up to occupy fortified farmhouses in the front line, relieving infantry who were withdrawn for training in preparation for the spring offensive. A Squadron Headquarters and each of its four troops occupied a separate farmhouse, protected by a minefield and a wire entanglement. The headquarters house was 600 yards back from the twenty-foot-high floodbank of the river Senio, which marked the front line from west of Faenza to the Comácchio lagoon on the Adriatic. The days were spent working on and improving the defences, and the nights in regular watches in case of a German raid, which never came. Indeed the chief enemy was boredom. At headquarters the long hours were enlivened by the presence of John Trimmer, a Queen's Bays officer doing a staff job but on temporary attachment to the regiment. Trimmer was a solicitor in civilian life and told many amusing anecdotes from his professional career. He claimed that his greatest legal triumph was his defence of a motorist charged with careless driving as a result of a night collision with a car parked on the Camberley to Farnborough road. The road was poorly lit by widely-spaced street lamps. These produced, John submitted, pools of light and pools of darkness, and on leaving a pool of light his client was temporarily blinded until his eyes became accustomed to the dark, causing him not to see the car parked at the roadside without lights. The magistrate accepted this argument, and John's client was acquitted.

The regiment not only relieved infantry in the Senio Line but also sent some tanks up to support the infantry holding that line. This was a situation very like what it must have been like on the Western Front in the First World War with both sides holding positions along the narrow Senio river, which was not much more than twenty feet wide. Since the Senio flooded in spring and autumn due to melting snow from the mountains or heavy rainfall, the river was protected by high floodbanks that could be up to thirty feet high and about ten feet wide at the top.

Back with the rest of the regiment after my fortnight's stint as infantry, I received a telephone call from Robert Crosbie-Dawson, formerly a Bays squadron leader but now on the staff of Eighth Army. He had been deputed to send an aircraft to Malta to buy supplies of drink for the mess of the army commander, Dick McCreery. Would I like to go as buyer, he asked, and, at the same time, take the opportunity to obtain supplies for the regiment? Naturally, I leapt at the chance, quickly obtained my commanding officer's permission and set off. The journey to Malta was uneventful. Since victory at El Alamein had freed Malta from the threat of invasion and constant air raids, a great deal had been done to clear the streets of the capital Valletta of rubble. A surprising number of buildings seemed to be intact. I established myself in the British club which, with very few members, was operating with all the conveniences of a London club, including waiters in tails. The next morning I began a systematic tour of the wine merchants, who were numerous because in peacetime they had had a thriving business supplying the Mediterranean Fleet and the Malta garrison. At each I met the English board of directors and received the same answer to my request: they had received no fresh supplies of drink for four years and their cellars were practically empty: however, as it was for the commander of their liberator the Eighth Army they would make a case of wine available from their meagre stores; there would, of course, be no charge. In this way I accumulated nine cases, of which I allocated six to the Army Commander's Mess and three to the regiment.

On the third morning I took a truck out to the airfield with my purchases, and found that the plane appointed to fly me back to Rimini was an Italian Savoia-Marchetti, an ancient two-engined machine whose fuselage looked as if it had been torn from the roof of a Nissen hut. Its normal use was dropping supplies to Yugoslav partisans, and its interior behind the cockpit was a totally bare space for stowing cargo. There was no passenger seat, and for the 600 miles flight I should have to perch precariously on one of the cases of wine. It was a windy day, and it did not seem a happy augury for a safe journey when I found the pilot, a cheerfully laconic Englishman, on the ground underneath the plane holding down a map of Italy torn from a school atlas with one hand and measuring the bearing for our route with a protractor with the other. It was hardly scientific navigation, especially as at least a third of the route was over the mountainous spine of Italy with peaks rising to 10,000 feet.

As soon as the pilot had finished planning the route we were off. The skies were clear over Sicily and the Tyrrhenian Sea, but as soon as we reached mainland Italy we ran into dense banks of cloud which blotted out all the view of the land beneath us. It was safe enough as long as we stayed aloft because we were flying high enough to clear the mountains, but how was the pilot to know that it was time to descend when the cloud banks remained unbroken. We flew on and on, for several hours, until at last a tiny gap appeared in the clouds and sea, obviously the Adriatic, was visible thousands of feet below. We were beyond the mountains, and the pilot did not lose a moment in putting the plane into a steep dive through the hole. Inside the aircraft there was chaos. The cases of wine slid violently down the floor to end up in a pile against the front partition, fortunately without breaking any bottles; and I was in agony. It felt as if my whole head was going to cave in, and I lay helplessly on the floor clutching my ears with both hands and sobbing with pain. Finally the plane levelled out a few hundred feet above the sea, the pilot did a left turn and we flew over the coast to our destination, which in the circumstances was surprisingly close.

Several days passed before the pain in my ears subsided. But they were pleased, at both army and regimental headquarters, with what I had brought them, and told me that I had done well. They did not know how lucky they had been to get anything at all.

The severe winter of 1944–45 was followed by an early, warm, dry spring. Soon leaves were on the trees. As if by magic nets, bats and balls appeared, and for a few days we seemed to be preparing for a cricket season. But this sporting interlude did not last. Within a few days we were moving up to play our part in the offensive that was to bring the war in Italy to an end. The first major objective was the Argenta Gap, a dead flat area of vineyards and orchards criss-crossed with irrigation and drainage ditches between the Comácchio lagoon and the river Reno with the town of Argenta at its centre. After Argenta it was on to the river Po, the greatest of Italian water obstacles if the Germans still had the will and the strength to defend it effectively.

I was still second-in-command of A Squadron under Jackie Harman, and my Sherman crew was the same as it had been for many months: driver Ned Lord, gunner Eddie Parish and Trooper Maidment. One evening early in the battle, when we were ready to move off in support of the infantry, Maidment and I were standing in the turret of the tank, heads and shoulders exposed, when a concentration of mortar fire fell on the squadron. The tanks were enveloped in black smoke and stones and mortar fragments rattled against the tank sides. When the smoke had cleared I looked across, and there was no sign of Maidment. I wondered what on earth could have happened to him: could he have been blown to pieces or lifted clean out of the tank by the force of an exploding mortar shell? At last I caught sight of him in the murky interior, on all fours down on the floor of the tank. 'What are you doing down there, Maidment?' I called out. 'I dropped my pencil, sir,' he answered.

We were supporting 38 (Irish) Brigade of 78th Division in the western and 11 Brigade of the same division in the eastern sector of the offensive on the Argenta Gap. There can have been no finer infantry in the British

Army than the Irish Brigade. The Irishmen regarded the purpose of a battle as not only killing Germans but collecting loot from prisoners. After one engagement in which we had supported the Royal Irish Fusiliers, commanded by Colonel Murphy Palmer, whose Irish brogue was inimitable, a groundsheet was laid out on which all the loot was displayed – mostly watches, but also cigarette lighters and other silver trinkets. How the loot was divided among the men was a mystery.

The performance of 56th (London) Division was a revelation. By the end of the autumn battles they had appeared exhausted and dispirited. It seemed that the months of training and replenishment had re-invigorated them.

One day squadron headquarters was in a farmhouse on the edge of a wide expanse of grassland when a battalion of 11 Brigade came through in extended order to continue the advance, and I noted that the men moved with a real sense of purpose that had been missing before. As darkness fell that evening a German soldier jumped down from an upstairs window of our farmhouse and ran across the fields towards the German lines before we could do anything to stop him. He had been hiding all day and, as we had had no occasion to go upstairs, we had never found him. He deserved to get clean away.

Later that evening I received the news from regimental headquarters that I was to go on leave to England, and immediately began my journey down the boot of Italy to take ship at Naples. We were somewhere in the Bay of Biscay when the news came through that Germany had capitulated and the war in Europe was over. My career as a combatant officer was finished. The infantry's baleful autumn 1944 syndrome was not confined to 56th Division. It was equally prevalent in our colleagues of 46th Division. Our platoon commander in that division confided that in an attack he was lucky if half a dozen of his men were with him he reached the objective though, once he was established there, more would join him in ones and twos. The persistent rain and the repetitive river line battles had eaten into the infantrymen's soul. Morale was not helped by the fact that once a soldier had become detached through wounding, sickness or other cause he lost all connection with his original regiment and became simply an infantry reinforcement, so all *esprit de corps*, all sense of regimental pride and loyalty, was lost. One evening on an approach march we stopped for shelter at a farmhouse and found a soldier with the insignia of the Lincolns hiding in a cellar. We handed him over to the Military Police. Three days later, when we were halted at the roadside, a column of the Leicesters marched past on their way to the front, with our would-be deserter in the midst of them.

The Irish regiments of 38 Brigade were different. They kept tabs on any member of the regiment who was wounded or went sick and made sure that he returned to his regimental home when he recovered. That was one of the secrets of their sky high morale.

The restoration of high morale throughout Eighth Army was largely due to the skilful leadership of Dick McCreery who had succeeded Leese as army commander in October 1944. By his careful handling of his infantry, and his deployment of armoured units to relieve the infantry in the line during the winter, he was able to build up the strength of the army and to restore its sense of purpose. Looking after soldiers' welfare in many ways, including arranging home leave to the UK, he had all but eliminated the problem of desertion that had afflicted Eighth Army in late 1944. He also instilled confidence in his soldiers so that they felt that the final push in Italy would lead to something tangible – the defeat of the German armies and the coming of peace.

Chapter Twelve

Post War

The unconditional surrender of all the German forces in Italy under von Vietinghoff had taken place on 2 May. By early June I was back with the regiment after a fortnight's leave in England. The regiment then was at Valdagno, a pleasant little town in a mountain valley north of Vicenza, which in turn was thirty miles west of Venice. The feature of Valdagno was a hotel-restaurant where they did a nice line in roast guinea fowl.

The regiment had acquired a number of horses captured from the Germans including one we had named Frederick Henry after the principal character in Hemingway's *A Farewell to Arms*. Frederick Henry was a big, common but, on the whole, docile bay which the latest-joined subaltern, Tony Cottam, begged to take out for a ride. One afternoon I was chatting with two brother officers, George Rich and Crash Keyworth, as we sat on our horses on the outskirts of Valdagno. There was a clatter of hooves down the road, and Frederick Henry appeared riderless at a gallop, stirrups flapping on his flanks and the inane expression on his face typical of a runaway horse. He continued past us without a pause, on towards the stables. A few minutes later he was followed by Tony, dishevelled and covered in dust, with a rent in his breeches and several grazes. 'Bloody Frederick Henry,' he muttered as he limped past us. He never asked to take him out on a ride again, and never explained how the normally tractable Frederick Henry had managed to get rid of him.

We did not stay in Valdagno long. There were alarming reports that the Yugoslav army, known to us colloquially as the 'Jugs', had designs on Trieste, the large port in the extreme north-east corner of Italy, and were contemplating an invasion to annex it. To counter this threat our forces were built up on the Italian side of the border with Yugoslavia. In accordance with this defensive plan the regiment was moved to the neighbourhood of Aiello, a village near the small walled town of Palmanova, thirty miles north-west of Trieste. Although the threat from the Jugs was taken seriously, it did not interfere with our daily rides, or laying down a polo ground, or, most importantly, constructing a racecourse at Aiello. The Jug invasion never came.

The early weeks at Aiello were my last of actual soldiering, as my energies were soon diverted to horse racing. Racing was adopted as an important leisure interest for the troops. Horses were plentiful, there were many officers who had been involved in racing in England before the war, and the sport received encouragement at the highest level. On the disbandment of Eighth Army, General Sir Richard McCreery had been appointed C-in-C British Troops in Austria and British High Commissioner in the Allied Commission for Austria. He had been a leading amateur over fences and had won the Grand Military Gold Cup at Sandown twice. He not only gave the organization of race meetings his blessing, but took part himself as an owner.

By the autumn of 1945 race meetings were being held at regular fortnightly intervals at four courses: at Treviso, a few miles north of Venice, and at Aiello in Italy; and at Klagenfurt and Graz in the British zone of Austria. Vienna's racecourse, the Freudenau in the Prater, the vast amusement park on the outskirts of the city, was in the Russian sector, Vienna being divided into four sectors administered by the British, the Russians, the Americans and the French respectively. However, Dick McCreery managed to persuade Marshal Konev, the Russian High Commissioner, to allow the British to hold a meeting at the Freudenau on 27 October, to which all the leading members of the Allied commissions were invited. Marshal Konev was one of the most distinguished Russian generals and was an acknowledged master of camouflage and deception; he had commanded the so-called 'Steppes Front' at the decisive battle of Kursk in 1943 and afterwards commanded the armies that smashed the German defence line on the Oder and opened the way to the capture of

Berlin. He clearly enjoyed the hot buffet lunch provided by Dick for his guests at the Freudenau, and equally clearly assumed that the result had been fixed when Dick's own horse Jumbo won the principal race of the day, the Champion Chase. Jumbo came with a strong run at the last fence, flew it in fine style and streaked away to win easily. He was ridden with great confidence by Joe Hartigan wearing Dick's own 'emerald green, black cap' colours which had been brought out from England especially for the occasion.

Jumbo's provenance is not known for sure. George Brown, who was Dick's ADC at the time, believes he was captured from the Germans, and this is probable because the German army, even at the end, was using much horsed transport and hundreds of horses were captured at the time of the German surrender. Many of them were thoroughbreds, or were at least partly thoroughbred, and were the large majority of our racehorse population in Austria and Italy. The other main source was the English hunters taken out to Palestine by the 1st Cavalry Division in the autumn of 1939 and brought to Italy by the Royal Army Veterinary Corps after the mechanization of that division. We had one of the Cavalry Division horses in our regimental racing string, a grand old chestnut, tough and honest, and one of the best chasers and stayers on the flat in the army racing, named Entertainer.

Jumbo was a big, powerful bay, and looked the part of a thoroughbred chaser. Whatever his origin may have been, he was a horse of note apart from his victory at Freudenau. Dick McCreery took him back to England and rode him with the Blackmore Vale hounds on the Somerset and Dorset borders when he was master and joint-master of that pack for several seasons. Dick's son Bob rode him in several point-to-points and won a race on him at the Wylye Valley. Bob attributes his decision to make a career in racing partly to his enthusiasm kindled by his win on Jumbo. The decision turned out extremely well. A very stylish and accomplished rider, Bob was champion amateur under National Hunt rules twice and became a successful breeder of horses for the flat with a highly respected place in the industry. Bob's success was Jumbo's legacy.

I did not have a ride at that Vienna meeting, and was a witness of Jumbo's victory merely as a spectator. But my return to the Prater and the Freudenau brought back memories of the summer of 1937 when I had been a PG of the von Zeidler family to learn German in the interval between leaving Wellington and going up to Cambridge. The von Zeidler family consisted of the general, an invariably courteous cavalry soldier who had fought at the disastrous battle of Lemberg in 1914, his wife, a Hungarian by birth, who was soft and sweet like strawberry jam, and their daughter Yolanda (Yoli), aged twenty-one and studying English at Vienna University, who was dark, attractive, coquettish and moody. I struck up a firm friendship with the general, and we went out on many small expeditions. He loved to reminisce about the good old days before the downfall of the Austro-Hungarian Empire. One day we were drinking a glass of beer in a cafe beside a road through the Prater when he began to describe what we would have seen if we had been sitting there on a Sunday race day before the Great War. It had been the custom of the fashionable Viennese to go out to the races in their carriages at a flat-out gallop, raising dense clouds of dust from the sandy tracks, and the more thickly covered with dust you were when you arrived at the Freudenau the smarter you were. On the course the ladies tossed their dust-laden veils back over their heads to reveal their unblemished faces. Frau von Zeidler enjoyed the races and we went there several times together. In the afternoons I often walked halfway to the University to meet Yoli; sometimes we would stop at a pavement ice-cream stall on the way home; they had many flavours that you did not find in England, and I usually chose apricot. In the von Zeidlers' flat the windows were kept shut and the curtains drawn all day to keep out the stifling summer heat. As the air cooled in the evening Yoli would throw open a window wide and recline in a low armchair in front of it, her arms held stiffly at her sides so that her breasts jutted firmly upwards inside her blouse, daring me, I thought, to fondle them. But I never touched her, and I never tried to kiss her. I was a gauche eighteen-year-old conditioned by the unnatural environment of all-male boarding schools.

On the morning after Jumbo's victory I decided to try and call on the von Zeidlers. They had seemed very old in 1937 and I thought it was unlikely that they had survived the war, but it was worth a try. I walked south from the Ringstrasse opposite the once ritzy but badly bombed Kartnerstrasse, past the baroque Karlskirche, then right into the Schleifmuhlgasse, and so to number 2, where their flat was on the second floor. I rang the bell, and a minute later the cover of a spy-hole slid back and an eye appeared, which I recognized at once as the general's. I heard him cry out in great surprise 'es ist der Peter', and a moment later the door was flung open and I was given the warmest of welcomes from the general and Frau von Zeidler. Yoli was absent. She had married late in the war and was marooned in communist Budapest. My welcome was indeed warm, but embarrassed, because they had nothing to offer me. They were terribly short of food. Rations were very meagre, and they were too old and infirm to get out and shop on the black market. They did not want me to stay but begged me to come back the next morning. I complied, and the next day was treated to a rather nasty paté whose ingredients I could not even guess at, spread on hard biscuits and washed down by cherry brandy. It was an attempt at hospitality pathetic enough to drive one to tears. I could do nothing for them, but when I returned to Vienna for a second race meeting the following June I brought them ham, a bag of flour, sugar, jam and butter, all of which were available, at a price, in Italy.

Jumbo's rider Joe Hartigan was only one of the individuals involved in the post-war army racing to play a part in the thoroughbred industry at home. He was the son of Frank Hartigan, who trained at Weyhill near Andover and had the reputation of a hard man and a harsh employer. Joe was the opposite in character. Pipe-smoking and easy-going, he had ridden winners as an amateur before the war and trained for a good many years after it but lacked the drive and ambition to do more than struggle on the lower rungs of the profession. Dick Hern was in a totally different category of trainer. He served in the North Irish Horse, who were stationed first at Rimini and then at Graz in the months following the end of the war. The regiment had runners at the meeting at the Freudenau in October 1945, but only Birdcatcher, ridden by Dick in a three-mile chase, ran into a place. The North Irish Horse moved to Germany at the end of 1945 and Dick was lost to army racing. He was demobbed in the autumn of 1946 and soon settled down to become one of the most successful trainers of Classic horses in the second half of the twentieth century. He won the Derby with Troy, Henbit, and Nashwan and trained the winners of thirteen other British Classic races including the so-called 'Horse of the Century', Brigadier Gerard. Another North Irish Horse officer, Michael Pope, a great friend of Dick, also rode at the early army meetings in Italy and Austria, and became a very successful trainer of horses on the flat. Lionel Vick, who rode winners at Treviso, was a moderately successful steeplechase jockey in the north of England until he broke his back in a fall; after recovering from his injuries but confined to a wheelchair, he trained as and became an accountant and looked after the tax affairs of large numbers of jockeys. John de Burgh, of the 16th/5th Lancers, and Tim Rogers, of the 4th Hussars, both rode winners in Austria and rose to positions of eminence in the Irish breeding industry. John inherited Oldtown, a rundown ancestral estate at Naas in County Kildare, and by sheer diligence and expertise, turned it into a thriving thoroughbred nursery. Tim, a son and brother respectively of the Classic trainers Darby and Mick Rogers, revolutionized Irish breeding by standing top-class stallion stations at his studs Airlie and Grangewilliam. Although surpassed subsequently as a stallion promoter by the Coolmore Stud under John Magnier, Tim had been the trailblazer and made a major contribution to the progress of Irish breeding with such great stallions as Habitat and Petingo.

My entry into the army racing world was as an officer in charge of the Bays' racing string, which consisted of half a dozen horses looked after by three soldier grooms. The horses were Top Hat, a thoroughbred purchased cheaply in Milan by George Rich and myself, the old English hunter Entertainer, three mares captured from the Germans – Maybe, Loppy and Ranee – and Outlook, a dapper chestnut of the Hanoverian breed who had a charming character but limited racing ability. I rode Top Hat in his first and only race, when he made all the running and was never off the bridle; unfortunately he was chronically lame and was never able to run again. Maybe was so-called because she was so round in the barrel when we acquired her that we thought she must be in foal; but however hard we worked her and raced her – and she ran with great regularity – she never lost her rotundity. She won several races on the flat and over fences. Crash Keyworth took her back to Ireland, where she quickly learnt to jump banks and carried him with great distinction in the hunting field. Loppy, descriptively but unimaginatively named before I had anything to do with her, was always a brilliant jumper but very weak in her early racing days and tended to fade away towards the end of her races. She improved rapidly in the summer of 1946 with the good feeding we were able to give her – there was an army ration which we supplemented with oats purchased from an Italian feed merchant. Ranee was far the best of the ponies racing there – ponies were defined as horses not more than 15 hands. She was very bloodlike, and I had easy wins on her at Klagenfurt and at the summer meeting at the Freudenau; and I was secretly rather pleased when a very young officer called Rodney Windsor, who had implored me to let him have the ride, was beaten into third place on her in a race at Graz. For the winter months, when racing was in Italy, I based the string with the regiment at Aiello, but in the summer months, when all the racing was on the Austrian courses, I moved the string and became a guest trainer with the 16th/5th Lancers who were idyllically stationed in a village on a trout stream twenty miles north of Klagenfurt.

I never had a ride at Treviso because I was too busy managing the meetings. It was a strange little course, almost circular with a circumference of six furlongs. The horses seemed to cope with the constant bends remarkably well. All the manual work was done by a PoW German captain with thirty German other ranks. They made no attempt to escape, considering their lot with generous British rations far preferable to life in devastated, starving Germany. They were even allowed to take a lorry up into the foothills of the Alps to collect birch for the fences. They did the work with typical German efficiency. The course was in marked contrast to Aiello, a mile-and-a-quarter circuit with a straight five-furlong tangential chute.

I had one other responsibility in the army racing world. I was the official handicapper. A handicap is a race in which the weights to be carried by the horses are adjusted for the purpose of equalizing their chances of winning and so spreading the fruits of victory more evenly in the racehorse population, and the handicapper is the person appointed to allot the weights. The handicapper has to make two assumptions: one, that past performances are a true reflection of the horse's ability; and two, that the horse will reproduce the same form in the future. Neither of these assumptions is necessarily realistic. If they were, and the handicapper did his work well and accurately, every handicap race should end in a multiple dead heat. This does not happen. These truths were brought home to me as a novice handicapper somewhat rudely.

Tim Rogers had been appointed as temporary ADC to Winston Churchill when the Prime Minister visited Egypt in August 1942, and they had become such firm friends that their association was renewed for all Winston's subsequent visits to the troops in the Mediterranean theatre. Consequently it was only natural for Tim to name the horse of considerable ability that he acquired Colonel Warden, the code name of the Prime Minister. Tim rode Colonel Warden in a race at Klagenfurt in which he finished a moderate third, and then entered him for a mile handicap, the chief race at the Vienna summer meeting. Naively, I assumed that Colonel Warden had shown his true form at Klagenfurt and weighted him accordingly. It was probably a stone less than he should have carried to reflect his real ability. He sailed in an easy winner and Tim, who had backed him at 6 to 1, made a large sum of money. His winnings were paid in worthless occupation *schillings* but, after smart manipulation of the exchanges, Tim was left with enough Italian *lire* to buy a villa on Lake Como.

My time in the army was drawing to a close, and I was due to be sent home to be demobbed at the end of September. My hopes for further riding successes were centred on Loppy. The other members of the string were fully exposed and hard to place with winning chances, but Loppy was improving almost day by day from a relatively low base. She was a lovely, compact mare, with quarters packed with muscle, and she was a superb jumper. I rode her in a novice chase at Klagenfurt in August, and she won comfortably after taking up the running at the turn into the straight. She was entered in another steeplechase at Klagenfurt on the day before I was to board the train for England at Spittal at the opposite, western end to Klagenfurt of the long, narrow and picturesque Wortersee. She had continued to improve visibly and I was confident of winning again and leaving army racing on a triumphant note. There were nine other runners, but only Grey Squirrel, owned by the 16th/5th Lancers and ridden by John de Burgh, had shown any worthwhile form. The race was over two miles, which meant we had a circuit and a half of the course to cover. We jumped off, and coming up the straight and past the winning post for the first time Loppy was going easily in fourth place. Past the winning post the course went over a steep mound with a sharp right-handed bend at the top, and then levelled out to meet a series of four fences down the far side. The three leaders ran wide round the bend and, without acceleration on Loppy, I found myself in front descending the slope towards the next fence. We were nearing the fence when I caught sight of Grey Squirrel out of the corner of my eye, coming with a violent swerve towards me from the outside of the course. There was a shattering collision which knocked Loppy clean off balance. She staggered the last few strides, could not gather herself for take-off, toppled over the fence and collapsed in a heap on the far side. I was thrown clear, and the remaining eight runners galloped over the top of me, most of them seeming to give me a kick for good measure as they passed. From my position on the ground I had a clear view across the course to see Grey Squirrel flying the last two fences and going on to win unchallenged by several lengths. I lay there for a while, bruised and a bit battered but not seriously hurt – Loppy was unhurt too – and wondering whether the collision had been accidental or intentional; a question to which I had no difficulty in guessing the answer. Then I got up and, like the pig in the popular song, slowly walked away.

In those days Tim Rogers and John de Burgh were more canny and more streetwise, in a racing sense, than I was. In civilian later life we all achieved positions of prominence in the racing world, and we became great friends. I never visited Ireland without staying a night or two with Tim Rogers at Airlie and John de Burgh at Oldtown. But in all our reminiscing and all our discussions on many different aspects of racing we never referred to Colonel Warden or Grey Squirrel.

At 6 o'clock on the morning of 26 December 1946 I left my home, South Cadbury House in Somerset, to drive to Wolverhampton, which then had a National Hunt course, to carry out my first assignment for *The Sporting Chronicle*. I worked for that daily racing paper for thirty-five years before taking early retirement. I would have been better off financially if I had waited for another two years when the paper went out of circulation, but I had had more than enough of the mind-chilling tedium of racing journalism. I had long been accumulating a variety of outside interests. A growing fascination with the breeding of the Thoroughbred had led me to write two long articles for different publications on that subject each week; and that in turn resulted in my appointment in 1964 as one of the three members of a Jockey Club committee under the chairmanship of the Duke of Norfolk whose terms of reference were to make recommendations on the general programme of races with special attention to the top-class horses. Those recommendations were of seminal importance for the future of British racing, and for more than a quarter of a century I served on a committee formed to implement them. Those two appointments had lifted me at a stroke out of the stultifying routines of daily reporting.

Other responsibilities quickly followed. I became consultant to two leading thoroughbred breeders, the Duke of Norfolk himself, and Louis Freedman, a property developer who purchased and carried on successfully the Cliveden Stud made famous by the Astor family. Both of them had their rewards at the highest level of racing. For the Duke of

Norfolk, and after his death for his widow Lavinia, and after her death for their daughter Anne Lady Herries, I had a hand in planning the breeding of Ragstone, winner of the Ascot Gold Cup; Moon Madness, winner of the St Leger; Sheriff's Star, winner of the Coronation Cup; and Celtic Swing, winner of the French Derby; and for Freedman, Polygamy, winner of the Oaks; and Reference Point, winner of the Derby, the St Leger and King George VI and Queen Elizabeth Stakes. All those races were designated either as Classics or otherwise races of paramount importance.

To win the Derby is the ultimate ambition of every British owner and breeder, so the victory of Reference Point in that race was a special triumph. It was on my recommendation that Freedman bought Byblis, a winner of two small races, for the moderate price of 6,000 guineas when he wanted to add a mare with upgrading prospects to his broodmare band. I chose Busted as a mate for her because he was a good influence for stamina and she was by Grey Sovereign, a speed specialist, and hopefully this mixture should produce a satisfactory balance of speed and stamina. In fact this mating over-egged the stamina element, because the produce, Great Guns, needed two miles to be seen to advantage. So for Great Guns I chose Habitat, the leading speed stallion of the day and, incidentally, at the Airlie Stud of Tim Rogers. The produce was Home On The Range, a top-class race mare who won five races as a three-year-old including the important Sun Chariot Stakes. We were getting close to our objective. Home On The Range was a big, robust mare who, for all her class, could not quite stay a mile and a half, the distance of the Derby. So the choice of mate for her was Mill Reef, a horse of medium build and great quality, a winner of the Derby himself and already the sire of Derby winner, Shirley Heights. The resulting produce was Reference Point. So in three generations we had achieved by selective breeding an upgrading from mediocrity to the summit of racing achievement.

Louis wrote to me in a letter after the Derby:

Obviously congratulations in some form are due to us but, although we appear in all the record books as owners and breeders of Reference

Point, neither Val [his wife] nor I are in any doubt that it was a team effort tracing back to purchasing the shares in Habitat, your advice to buy Byblis and swopping Mill Reef (sire of Reference Point). You can be in no doubt that Val and I are grateful and thank you for the vital role you play in planning our matings so skilfully.

Louis was a man who rose to the top of every enterprise he espoused. He was chairman of Land Securities, one of the biggest property companies, and chairman also of the Race Relations Board and numerous health authorities, being appointed CBE for his services to race relations. In racing he was at different times President of the Racehorse Owners Association and Deputy Senior Steward of the Jockey Club. He was a generous and loyal friend. Above all he was transparently honest. Financial shortcuts and evasions were totally alien to his nature and thinking. Accordingly he was deeply shocked when in 1988 an article in *The People* alleged that he has been party to an illicit deal in respect of the retainer paid to Lester Piggott, the first jockey to Reference Point's trainer Henry Cecil, for the purpose of avoiding tax. Louis brought an action for libel against the newspaper, and asked me to be a witness as to character on his behalf. I of course agreed.

I spent an hour with Louis's solicitor in his London office answering questions, all about myself and my career. Two days later the solicitor rang me up at home and questioned me for a further hour, all the questions again being about myself. In the end I lost patience and interrupted him, saying: 'I was asked to give evidence as to Louis's character, but all you do is ask me about myself'. 'Oh yes.' he replied. 'But first I have to establish your credibility.'

The case came to court. On the third day, the eve of my scheduled appearance in the witness box, the defence accepted defeat. Louis was awarded heavy damages and costs, and his reputation was overwhelmingly vindicated. Nevertheless, the case had been a traumatic experience for Louis, and his relationship with the racing world never fully recovered its former easy pattern.

In 1981 I was elected a member of the Jockey Club, then the governing body of British racing. I served a five-year term as President of the Thoroughbred Breeders Association, and two terms as a director of the National Stud. I was a director of Goodwood, one of the premier racecourses and certainly the most beautiful, for thirty-two years, and was the author of eight books on racing and breeding subjects. In 1984 the European Breeders Fund was formed to channel money from stallion owners into much needed race prize money for the support of the racing industry, and I was appointed chairman of the British section of the Fund, a post which I held for twelve years. Over the course of time I received five awards for services to the racing and breeding industries, the last being the *Daily Telegraph* Award of Merit in the Cartier Racing Awards, the most prestigious award made to an individual. I had one venture outside the confines of the racing world when in June 1966 I read a paper on 'The British Racehorse Breeding Industry' at the Royal Society of Arts at the Society's house in John Adam Street in Adelphi. In the paper I referred to the unsoundness that was endemic in the racehorse. During the discussion that followed I was asked by Carey Foster, an Epsom vet who had come to prominence as Winston Churchill's racing manager, to what specific kind of unsoundness I was referring, with the obvious intention of exposing me as an ignorant impostor. I was saved by the intervention of the eminent Irish vet J. S. M. Cosgrove, who stated, 'As a veterinary surgeon I should like to speak in support of Mr Willett's observations on the question of unsoundness in the racehorse.' Such expert support silenced Carey Foster. Afterwards I was awarded the Society's Silver Medal and appointed a Fellow of the Society, so presumably my paper was considered to have some merit.

My most far-reaching influence arose from the report of the Norfolk Committee. It was at my insistence (at my insistence because Norfolk was a poor wordsmith and included any memo I sent him in the report; while Geoffrey Freer, the only other member of the committee, was the most respected sage of the Turf, but made only a disappointing contribution to the proceedings. He died less than two years later, and must have been in failing health at the time) that the following sentence was included in the report: 'The Turf Authorities must ensure that a series of races over the right distances and at the right time of year are available to test the best horses of all ages …' This was the germ of the Pattern race system adopted not only in Great Britain but in every country in which horse racing is established, and sets the standard by which the best horses are judged.

Nearly all these activities took place long after I had retired from the army and the Territorial Army. But I am convinced that none of them would have come about but for the experience I gained, the contacts I made and the orientation I derived from the army racing in Italy and Austria immediately after the Second World War.

Retiring from the Bays did not mean a permanent end to my connection with the Army. One day in the summer of 1947, I was walking down Piccadilly when I encountered Peter Gill, who had been one of my fellow troop leaders in A Squadron of the Bays at Second Alamein. Peter had just been appointed Adjutant of the City of London Yeomanry (Rough Riders) and was busy recruiting officers for that re-formed regiment. He lost no time in enlisting me.

The Rough Riders were a yeomanry regiment formed in the Second Boer War, and had performed various roles in the meantime. They had seen active service in North Africa and Italy during the Second World War as a light anti-aircraft unit, and were now being re-formed as a Territorial armoured regiment. The regiment was affiliated to The Bays, who provided all the permanent staff; that accounted for the presence of Peter Gill and Daniel Asquith, my last commanding officer in The Bays and my first commanding officer in the Rough Riders. I was seeing familiar faces.

The Rough Riders had their headquarters and drill hall near Bedford Square, between the Tottenham Court Road and Gower Street. Drill nights, when individual training was undertaken, was on Wednesdays. We had occasional weekend exercises at Aldershot and other military centres, and a two-week annual camp, sometimes as far afield as Castlemartin in Pembrokeshire. The atmosphere on training weekends and at camp was relaxed, and consumption of alcohol in the Officers' Mess was on a generous scale.

Daniel Asquith was succeeded as commanding officer by Ronnie Shaw-Kennedy, a civilized bachelor, thickset with a slightly straggly moustache and a strong sense of humour, who lived in a luxurious flat in Mount Street, W1. He enjoyed good food and, on Wednesday nights after training, he and I used to take the short walk across Tottenham Court Road to the White Tower, an excellent Greek Cypriot restaurant, in Percy Street. Ronnie loved a heavily retsinated wine they kept there called the Duke of Sparta and we always had a bottle with our dinner. Ronnie was insistent that I should read Marcel Proust's *Remembrance of Things Past*. 'I will lend you the first two volumes, and when you have finished them you can bring them back and I will lend you the next two, and so on until you have read all twelve', he told me. It took me four weeks to read the first seventy pages, but then I took off, and finished the two volumes in a few more days. I took them back to Ronnie and told him, 'I don't want to borrow any more. I have been down to Hatchards' [the famous bookshop in Piccadilly] and bought a complete set for myself.' From that time on I was an ardent Proustian.

Ronnie loved poetry and literature. On one exercise I came across him standing in the turret of his tank with a volume of Keats' poems open on the turret flap in front of him.

I resigned from the Rough Riders in 1953. I had just got married and considered it unreasonable to have regular absences from home for drill nights, weekends and camps. I had had five years in a regular regiment and six years in a territorial regiment and that really did bring my connection with the Army to an end.

Chapter Thirteen

The Racing Years

My fascination with horse racing had begun at a very early age. I have a clear recollection of lying on my tummy on the drawing-room floor with the racing page of *The Times* open in front of me, and wondering what on earth was meant by 'Probable Starters and Jockeys'. I was six years old and had just learnt to read. In the twenty-first century runners for flat races have to be declared forty-eight hours before the date of the race. In the 1920s entries for flat races closed several weeks before the date of running, but runners did not have to be declared until forty minutes before the time of the race. So lists of probable starters and their riders were compiled by the Press Association and published on the sporting pages of all daily newspapers. This procedure gave me, as a six-year-old, much food for thought.

The next stage of my initiation into the ways of horse racing was when my father took me, aged eight, to a meeting at Plymouth, a course now long defunct. I picked the winner of a hurdle race, Wadi Halfa, and my father backed it for me at 8 to 1, but memories of the day were not all happy. The weather was hot and sunny, and our Humber's hood was down, enabling a thief to snatch the handbag of my sister-in-law to be from the back seat, to her tearful distress. In the 1930s my family had a cottage on Dartmoor where we spent summer holidays, which allowed my father and I to attend the jumping meetings at Newton Abbot, a course which still flourishes, and Totnes, where racing terminated at the outbreak of the Second World War. I followed closely the fortunes of the horses trained by my Uncle Bob, my father's younger brother, who had a stable of about thirty jumpers at Pyecombe on the London road just outside Brighton. Most of his horses were of modest ability, but over the years he had a few good ones: like Gomar, who once beat the mighty Golden Miller, a true champion who won the Cheltenham Gold Cup five times, in a race at Sandown; the brilliant jumper of fences Sidmouth, who was still winning races at the advanced age of sixteen; and Drakensberg, an exceptionally handsome bay horse whose will to win did not fully match his inherent ability. My favourite was Guerrillero, a sweet little grey horse with a pronounced Arab profile. He was afflicted by nerves, and would shake violently while being saddled for a race, but managed to win a few times. When at Wellington College I used to walk down to Smith's, the stationers, in Crowthorne after lunch on Saturdays and buy the *Sporting Chronicle Handicap Book*, a publication which printed all the race entries for the following week, and spend the evening ticking off Uncle Bob's horses and calculating their chances.

Due to the proximity of the West Country courses, my interest in Uncle Bob's stable and my father's own preference, I was mainly a follower of steeplechasing and hurdle racing in my school days. That changed when I became an undergraduate at Cambridge University, which is only thirteen miles from Newmarket, the headquarters of flat racing. During my first two years at Cambridge I never missed a day's racing at Newmarket if I could help it. My third and final year was after the outbreak of war, when racing was greatly curtailed. But my interest was undiminished and, as recorded earlier in this work, served to endear me to the officers of A Squadron of the Queen's Bays when I joined the regiment in June 1941.

I was out of England, apart from a short period of leave in the spring of 1945, for five years from September 1941. It was thanks entirely to my father that I kept in touch with racing during that long absence. He had an antiquated and rickety machine on which he used to type all the previous week's racing results – there were seldom more than two or three meetings a week during the war – onto an air-mail letter card, the standard means of communicating with troops abroad. The lines of typing were so close that they were almost touching so as to make the maximum use of the available space and accommodate all the results; the receipt of those air-mail letter cards was a real boon for me.

In consequence I was well up-to-date with racing when I left the army, and reasonably qualified for a career on the Turf.

I have the impression that the members of the racing press in the twenty-first century are, as a body of men and women, sober, industrious and well-informed. It has to be no more than an impression, not a certainty, because I have been out of the mainstream of the industry since the millennium. But, impression or certainty, they contrast favourably with their forerunners when I entered racing more than sixty years ago. The racing journalists of that era were notorious for insobriety, indolence and a general lack of civilized priorities.

There were, of course, exceptions – like Eric Rickman of the *Daily Mail*, who was always dressed correctly for the occasion, whether it was Royal Ascot or Cheltenham, and observed strict standards of deportment. He was down like a ton of bricks on the Press Association reporter Dai Davies for appearing on the press balcony at Goodwood with a ham sandwich and a cup of tea. Such behaviour, he insisted, was undignified and unprofessional.

Ken Bryceson was more typical of the racing press of that era, though a first glance could be deceptive. He had served in the Royal Artillery during the Second World War, and was very proud of the fact; he always wore a gunner tie with his grey pinstripe suit. However, a second glance would reveal that the gunner tie was somewhat frayed and the suit jacket slightly threadbare at the elbows. He had attached himself to one of the Sunday papers, but never seemed to file any copy. During one summer heatwave I found myself walking into Goodwood racecourse from the car park with him. I remarked that it was hot. 'Hot, old boy,' exclaimed Ken. 'Why, I started to mow the lawn this morning and after one length of the lawn I had to sit down in a deck chair and have a gin and tonic.'

For one Grand National meeting he travelled by train to Liverpool with his friend Stuart Combe, who worked for another Sunday paper. It was a three-day meeting at Aintree on the outskirts of the city, but Bryceson and Combe never got nearer to Aintree than the bar of the Adelphi Hotel in the middle of Liverpool and missed the Grand National, the greatest steeplechase in the world. Ken was mild-mannered and always polite. That could not be said of all his colleagues. Frank Harvey, the veteran correspondent of the *Sunday Despatch*, was made of coarser material – Harris tweed to Ken's worsted. One day at the July course at Newmarket I was working at my desk in the Press Room when Frank appeared in front of me. He stood still, swaying slightly, for perhaps half a minute. Then he slowly raised his right hand until his forefinger was pointing at me accusingly, and said, 'You bastard. I've been watching you. You bastard.' Without another word he turned and tottered away. When he sobered up he must have repented of his rudeness and resolved to make amends, because the next day he appeared in front of me again, standing steady as a rock, and solemnly and silently handed me a choc bar.

Norman Pegg was the long-serving correspondent of one of the tabloids. A rotund, red-faced heavyweight, he could boast of a fine war record. He won the Military Medal (MM) with the Glosters on the Piave when the British troops were sent to stem the Italian rout after the Battle of Caporetto in 1917. Every year before the Derby in June he questioned me as to the prospects on breeding of the leading candidates staying the distance of one and a half miles. 'Breeding is not my business. Stories are my business,' he used to tell me. His tone implied that knowledge of breeding was inferior to the collection of news stories, like geese to swans. What he never explained was why breeding, if a factor to be taken into account in making a selection for the Derby, was not his business.

As my racing horizons began to broaden so did my concern with the idiosyncrasies of my Press Room colleagues diminish. The characters of leading trainers came more into focus and annual visits to their stables as the new season approached became routine. Noel Murless, who had nineteen English and Irish Classic victories including the Derby with Crepello, St Paddy and Royal Palace to his name when he retired in 1976, was the most successful trainer of top-class horses in his day, and his stable, Warren Place at Newmarket, was a regular annual destination. Noel was welcoming; he and his Scottish wife Gwen were hospitable, and I was usually invited to stay the night before going out to see the first lot on the gallops the next morning. Noel had made his way through the ranks – from moderate steeplechase rider, to successful trainer of ordinary horses at Hambleton in Yorkshire, to trainer of high-class horses at the famous Wiltshire stables at Beckhampton where the great Fred Darling had held court, to Turf headquarters, Newmarket. His training methods had evolved in the course of that odyssey; whereas at Hambleton he made his name by skilful placing of the largest possible number of his horses to win in their appropriate class, at Warren Place he showed disdain for mediocrity and concentrated his attention on the small number of his horses that he thought capable of attaining high class. His winners to horses in training ratio was risible. He could never accept that I, as a mere journalist, could have anything constructive to offer on the subject of race planning. Although, as a member of the Duke of Norfolk's Committee and the subsequent Pattern Committee, I had a shared responsibility for providing opportunities for the best horses, Noel's discussions of the subject always featured the activities of a nebulous 'they', never 'you'. He never saw an inch beyond the careers of the horses in his stable at the time. One year, at the time of my spring visit, he had two high-class four-year-old milers in his charge, but when I asked him if he had any running plans for them he shrugged and said, 'How could I? There are no races for milers of their class.' For the next season we promoted the Lockinge Stakes over a mile to Group 1, the highest category, but Noel had no top-class milers in his stable. He commented, 'I don't know what they want to promote a race like the Lockinge for.' He had no interest in anything that happened beyond the walls of his own stable yard, and always left the racecourse as soon as his horse, or horses, had run, no matter how important the races that were still to be contested.

At Warren Place it was necessary to proceed round the house in a somewhat gingerly fashion as his terriers would not neglect an opportunity to give your heels a nip. On one occasion he announced with pride that they had bitten three duchesses in a day.

Noel had a sharp, and sometimes cruel, wit. In 1974 Dibidale, ridden by Willy Carson and trained by Barry Hills, was deprived of victory in the premier fillies' Classic race, the Oaks, when her saddle slipped round under her belly in the final stages. At that time Barry was seldom seen without a large cigar in his mouth, though he later gave up smoking. Noel commented, 'No wonder Dibidale's saddle slipped. I don't suppose Barry could see the hole in the girth through the clouds of cigar smoke.' That incident was an example of the way luck can even itself up in racing. Polygamy had been beaten by the narrowest of margins in the first of the fillies' Classic races, the 1000 Guineas, after being nearly knocked over a furlong from the finish, but it was Polygamy who benefited from Dibidale's misfortune in the Oaks. Dibidale got her revenge in the Irish Oaks a month later.

Noel's treatment of owners was sometimes cavalier. One day he was taking a party of owners round evening stables. He slid back the door on one American barn, but quickly slid it to again, saying, 'We won't bother with those; they're all going to be sold.' But one owner had caught a glimpse of a familiar shape over Noel's shoulder, and blurted out, 'Isn't that old So-and-So in there,' naming one of his horses. 'Yes.' 'I didn't know he was going to be sold.' 'Well he is,' Noel told him.

One owner with whom Noel had an affectionate relationship was Louis Freedman, whose property company Ravenseft Properties played a prominent part in the rebuilding of the centres of war-devastated cities like Plymouth. When an immediate purchaser had to be found for the bloodstock interests of Lady Sassoon, Noel, who trained for her – he had won the Derby for her late husband Sir Victor with Crepello and St Paddy – knew which way to turn. 'I knew that Louis was the only person who could and would find the money at short notice,' Noel told me. The intervention of Noel and Louis saved the day for Lady Sassoon, and enabled the growing bloodstock empire of Louis Freedman to go forward on a broader front.

In later years Noel may have developed a few rough edges to his personality, but he was also capable of acts of extraordinary kindness and thoughtfulness. Once on my way to visit him I had a tyre blow out. After changing the wheel on a busy main road with cars and lorries thundering past seemingly within inches of my back, I arrived a little late for tea, and told my story. Noel made no comment, and having finished his tea got up and left the room without saying a word. He was away for at least half an hour, but when at last he returned he told me, 'I've sent that wheel of yours down to the garage to have a new tyre fitted. You probably have not got much money with you' – this was before the days of universality of plastic money – 'so don't pay me now. You can send me a cheque when you get home.' When it came to the development of the ability of a top-class racehorse, of course, Noel had no superior.

There is no such animal as a typical trainer. They come in all shapes and sizes, armed with a miscellany of qualities and prejudices. Some are congenital optimists, others are dyed in the wool pessimists. The most extreme optimist I met was Michael Blackmore in the 1950s. One Cesarewitch day at Newmarket I found myself walking into the course from the car park with him. The Cesarewitch is the most hotly contested long distance handicap of the year; it always attracts a big field, and there are many fancied runners. On this occasion Blackmore had a runner in the race, and I remarked that it must have a chance. He stopped, turned towards me and, leaning slightly forward for emphasis, stated categorically, 'My dear fellow. He'll not only win; he'll win easily.' The horse finished sixth of the thirty runners.

Tim Forster, on the other hand, was the archetypal pessimist. A former officer in the 11th Hussars, he had great charm and an intense love of horses in general, hunting and steeplechasers. He hated flat racing and despised hurdling, but had a consuming passion for racing over fences. He won the Grand National with Well to Do, Ben Nevis and Last Suspect, and trained such top-class chasers as Royal Marshall, Dublin Flyer and Martha's Son. But if his ingrained pessimism had rubbed off on his horses he would never have won the lowliest race in the Calendar.

Ben Nevis had gained two victories in the Maryland Hunt Cup, the most hazardous and prestigious race over jumps in the United States, but when his American amateur rider Charlie Fenwick was mounting him for the Grand National Tim offered one piece of advice, 'Keep remounting.'

It was not so much optimism as steely determination that saw Dick Hern through. Dick, who served with distinction in the tanks of the North Irish Horse in North Africa and Italy, was a pioneer of army racing in northern Italy in the months following the end of the Second World War. On leaving the army in 1946 he graduated through the jobs of riding instructor, event rider, assistant trainer and private trainer to the stature of full public trainer at West Ilsley at the end of 1962. He became one of the great trainers of Classic horses of the second half of the twentieth century, and by the time he retired in 1997 he had been responsible for no fewer than sixteen English Classic winners including the Derby winners Henbit, Troy and Nashwan. His career was not without accident or controversy. A keen hunting man, he broke his neck in a fall when out with the famous Shire pack, the Quorn, in December 1984, but continued to train from a wheelchair for thirteen more seasons.

Dick is not the only man to have trained successfully from a wheelchair. By a strange coincidence one of the others, Dick Gooch, trained at West Ilsley between the two world wars after breaking his back in a fall with the Quorn. But no chairbound trainer in Great Britain has achieved the same degree of success at the highest level as Dick. He had one asset that gave him a decisive advantage – his marvellous eyesight and powers of observation, of which I became aware when I was working on his authorized biography in 1999. I used to make frequent visits to West Ilsley, where he was still living at the Old Rectory, to discuss progress. There always were other visitors, and up to a dozen of us, often including his late wife's cousin Giles Blomfield and his great friend and business secretary Liz Brown, would sit down to lunch. Dick sat at one end of the long dining-room table and at one lunch session he suddenly interrupted the conversation, calling out to Giles at the far end, 'Watch out for that cream jug.' From five yards away, in the midst of a conversation of his own, he had noticed a tiny drip of cream about to fall from the lip of the jug.

He applied the same uncanny sense to his training. He could not feel horses' legs, the standard way of detecting incipient lameness, but he could see defects invisible to the normal human eye. Each day at evening stables he had the horses paraded in front of him, seated in his wheelchair, and picked out any soundness problem requiring rest or treatment. A less gifted man, as a tetraplegic, could never have coped with the complexities of training a string of high-class horses or satisfied the aspirations of demanding owners.

My connection with Bernard, 16th Duke of Norfolk, as a result of the Pattern of Racing Committee, led to an invitation to act as a consultant on his breeding affairs, with special responsibility for the choice of stallions for mating with his mares. At that time – 1966 – he had up to twenty-five mares at the Angmering Park Stud three miles up the A27 from his home at Arundel Park. We became firm friends, and from the end of that decade I was a regular guest at Arundel Park, not only for visits to the stud but for race meetings at the nearby courses, Goodwood and Brighton. The Duke had the post of Her Majesty's Representative at Ascot which gave him overall control of Ascot racing and also the use of a comfortable house within the bounds of the racecourse. I was a regular guest for race meetings there too.

One day in the summer of 1977 I was called to the telephone during dinner at Arundel Park. The caller was the Earl of March, son of the Duke of Richmond, the owner of the Goodwood estate and racecourse just six miles from Arundel. Lord March was the chairman of the racecourse, and the purpose of his call was to invite me to join the Goodwood Racecourse Board. I replied that, with great regret, I had to refuse the invitation; I explained that we had an unwritten rule on the Pattern Committee that members should have no commitment to any individual racecourse because of a possible conflict of interest. When I returned to the dinner table the Duchess asked me, 'Who was that?' I told her about Lord March's invitation, that I had refused, and the reason why. 'What a lot of nonsense,' she exclaimed. 'I'll go and tell him you'll do it.' Lavinia Norfolk was not a person to be readily gainsaid. I joined the Goodwood Board the following winter, and remained on it for thirty-two years. In the event no objection was ever raised to my membership of both the Pattern Committee and the Goodwood Board, and from that time on the unwritten rule was honoured only in the breach. They were momentous years at Goodwood. When I retired at the end of 2009 the implementation of a far-reaching modernization programme meant that, of the racecourse stands and buildings that had existed in 1978, only one, a stand in the cheapest enclosure, had not been replaced, while the parade ring and paddock had been re-positioned and levelled at the back of the Grandstand. I had also become a close friend of the chairman, who had succeeded to the title of Duke of Richmond, and a regular guest of the Duke and Duchess for race meetings.

Bernard, 16th Duke of Norfolk, as hereditary Earl Marshal, had the duty of organizing state occasions, which he did with impressive solemnity and dignity and, when there was marching to be done, as there was at the funeral of Sir Winston Churchill, literally with measured tread. Everything at the funeral, as it was at other state occasions like the coronations of King George VI and Queen Elizabeth and of Queen Elizabeth II, and the Investiture of the Prince of Wales, was planned and rehearsed with meticulous care and timing. He managed Ascot with the same attention to detail. When on duty his concentration never wavered. His public persona was pompous, impassive and unbending. At leisure, with friends or family, he knew how to relax and there was often a twinkle in his eye.

He loved Ascot and was devoted to its interests. For him the Gold Cup, Ascot's greatest race and the supreme test of stamina in the Thoroughbred, was the most coveted prize of all, far above any Classic or other famous race. So when his home-bred horse Ragstone won the Gold Cup in 1974 he had achieved a lifetime's ambition and his joy was unbounded. He was in tears as he greeted Ragstone after his victory and the crowd gathered round the winner's enclosure to cheer him to the echo.

He did not live into old age. He suffered a heart attack during a shooting party on the estate of Jim Joel, another prominent owner-breeder of racehorses, at Childwick Bury near St Albans and, although he recovered sufficiently to resume his duties at Ascot, he died on 1 January 1975, four weeks before his sixty-seventh birthday. During his last illness I was the only person outside the family allowed to visit him in his improvised sick-room in a ground-floor wing of Arundel Park, and I had a privileged place at his funeral in Arundel Cathedral. Lord Wigg, a former chairman of the Horserace Betting Levy Board and a fierce critic of Bernard in his lifetime, paid this generous tribute to him in the House of Lords, 'He was a man of great honesty of purpose who saw his duty and did it to the best of his ability. He never dissembled, and to such a man much may be forgiven.'

Bernard never shirked any task that he was set. For example, when Winston Churchill invited him to become Joint Parliamentary Secretary to the Minister of Agriculture in February 1941, he accepted instantly, saying, 'I have rather mixed feelings, but I don't think one should refuse.' It was a responsible and exacting post which he held until the end of the war. On the other hand he did not involve himself with the intricacies of racing form, though he was a keen horseman and hunting man in his youth and was Master of the Holderness Hounds for two seasons. He left the affairs of his racing stable to his wife Lavinia. A stepdaughter of the 6th Earl of Rosebery, a leading owner-breeder who won the Derby with Blue Peter and Ocean Swell, Lavinia was steeped in racing lore and was a skilful rider herself who hunted regularly with the renowned Beaufort Hounds. She had a deep understanding of racing form and knew as much about training the racehorse as most professionals. At the outbreak of the Second World War their horses were being trained privately by Victor Gilpin at Michel Grove on the Arundel estate, but when Gilpin joined the army the horses were moved to Arundel Park. There they were officially trained by Fred Bancroft, but it was an open secret that Bancroft was the head lad and most of the functions of trainer were carried out by Lavinia. In those days women were not permitted to hold a trainer's licence. By the time I became a regular visitor the dynamic John Dunlop was well established, Castle Stables was a public stable patronized by many owners besides the Norfolks, and Lavinia no longer played any part in the training operation. She did, however, still take a keen interest in the welfare and training of their horses. When I was staying there I would join her in her study at 7.30am, when she would already have dealt with her considerable mail. We would then walk the three-quarters of a mile to the top of the park, where the first lot of fifty horses would be circling under the trees under the watchful eye of John Dunlop after their first canter. After that, if it was a work morning, we would walk down to watch the horses gallop in pairs on the all-weather track on the east side of the park before going back to the house for breakfast. Lavinia's comments on the horses were always knowledgeable and illuminating.

She had a few odd idiosyncrasies. She was a chocoholic. For weeks, months even, she would not touch a chocolate; then one day she would eat her way through a whole box of expensive chocolates. She often ate nothing at breakfast, but after everyone else had left the room she would make her way round the table, eating all the left-over pieces of toast which she spread with butter and marmalade. She had the reputation of being a heavy bettor on horses, but I have no idea whether this was true. In the course of the years we discussed many and varied subjects, including intimate family details, but betting was never mentioned. Like Bernard, she was extremely public-spirited. She was involved with 150 charities, was an active supporter of them all and chairman or president of many. She gave frequent cocktail parties in Arundel Park in recognition of the contribution of individual supporters to Sussex charities. In 1990 she was appointed Lord Lieutenant of West Sussex, and was the first non-royal woman to be appointed to such a post. In her hands the Lord Lieutenancy was no sinecure. She took her responsibilities very seriously, attending every court in the county at least once and paying courtesy visits to many factories and businesses.

As a widow she maintained the family stud and horses in training interests with enthusiasm, but necessarily on a much smaller scale than

Bernard had done. Her greatest racing success, and only victory in a Classic race, was with Moon Madness in the St Leger at Doncaster in 1980. Moon Madness was a beautiful, dark bay in colour with a charming temperament. He made rapid improvement throughout his three-year-old season, first coming into prominence at Royal Ascot when he annihilated the field to win the King George V Handicap by five lengths. He was unluckily beaten in the Great Voltigeur Stakes at York in August, but everything went smoothly at Doncaster where he was in command two furlongs from the finish and galloped on in the hands of Pat Eddery to win by four lengths. The race coincided with a meeting at Goodwood, and, thanks to the kindness of the Duke of Richmond, I flew to Doncaster from Goodwood aerodrome by single-engined plane for the day. The skies were clear for the journey north, and for the return journey until we reached the line of the Thames, where we ran into dense cloud for the rest of the way. Goodwood aerodrome is immediately south of the Downs, which rise to 206 feet a mile from it. With visibility practically nil, I was nervous that we might begin our descent too soon and fly straight into the hill. I should have had more confidence in my pilot; when we levelled out below cloud level we were directly above the airfield, and landed with perfect safety.

Although Moon Madness was a very high-class horse, he was not the best horse bred by Lavinia Norfolk; the best was certainly Celtic Swing. When the stallions to cover the mares in the 1991 breeding season had to be selected Lavinia instructed me that money was tight and as little as possible was to be spent on stallion nominations. Accordingly, for Celtic Ring, a granddaughter of the brilliantly fast Fotheringay, I chose Damister, who in his racing days had finished third in the Derby without impressing the critics as a potential Classic sire, and stood for the affordable stud fee of £6,000. The produce of this mating was Celtic Swing, who developed into a great racehorse, officially rated the champion two-year-old of Europe in 1994 on the strength of his twelve-length victory in the *Racing Post Trophy*, one of the principal races for two-year-olds. The next year he won the French Derby, though by then he was showing signs of leg trouble and was not relatively as good as he had been as a two-year-old.

The prowess of Celtic Swing exceeded all reasonable expectations and emphasized the part that luck often plays in bloodstock breeding. Sadly Lavinia did not profit fully from his supreme athletic ability. In the spring of his two-year-old season, Peter Savill, who was enjoying a brief spell at the helm of British racing, paid a visit to the stable of Lavinia's daughter, Anne Lady Herries, at Angmering Park where Celtic Swing was in training. He was accompanied by his stable jockey, Kevin Darley, who rode Celtic Swing in a gallop and was so impressed that he strongly advised Savill to buy him. Thus Celtic Swing changed hands, though he stayed with Anne Herries and was trained by her throughout his racing career. By then Lavinia was in declining health and died in December 1995, just six months after the victory of Celtic Swing in the French Derby.

Celtic Swing was a true champion, and probably as a two-year-old the best horse to be trained in England for half a century. He had striking good looks, was powerfully built with quality, standing over a lot of ground and possessing an immense stride. He was in fact a black horse, with a white blaze and one white foot but, on account of an irrational prejudice against black horses in racing circles, he figures in the racing records as brown.

Moon Madness provided one of the ten victories in British Classic races, which included the Derby with Shirley Heights in 1978 and Erhaab in 1994, gained by his trainer John Dunlop. John's training methods had several noteworthy features. When the Norfolks' racing string was moved to Arundel Park many trees were felled and grass gallops opened up, but when the stable went public and horse numbers increased – at the zenith of his fortunes John trained 200 horses – the grass gallops were totally inadequate to stand the pounding of so many hooves. An all-weather canter and all-weather gallop were installed, and the grass training grounds were dispensed with altogether. From that time Arundel-trained horses seldom galloped on grass except when they ran in races. John had amazing mental powers of storing and disseminating information which enabled him to sit on his hack in front of a crowd of spectators and name without hesitation each of fifty horses cantering past in front of him in single file, often throwing in additional titbits of information as they passed.

The later stages of John's career were clouded by misfortune. At Christmas in 2000 he suffered a burst aneurysm in his aorta. He was rushed to Chichester Hospital where, by a stroke of luck, the one heart surgeon capable of performing the operation to save him was present and available. That saved his life. Even so, he was on the critical list for three weeks before beginning the slow progress to complete recovery. But the halcyon days were past. Horse numbers fell precipitately; in 2012 there were only sixty-seven horses in Castle Stables and it was not a viable proposition to train so few with the overheads of a much larger stable. In September of that year John was compelled to put his business into voluntary liquidation and retire from training.

John was one of the best, most intelligent and most successful trainers of his time. His score of Classic victories alone would be enough to secure a lasting place in the annals of the Turf. However another, at the time seemingly insignificant, achievement may have had even more momentous consequences. In June 1977 he saddled Hatta to win for Sheik Mohammed at Brighton. It was a race of no importance, but it was the Sheikh's first success and it fired the enthusiasm of the sheikh and the Maktoum family for racing in Great Britain. The vast Maktoum bloodstock empire that has developed has revolutionized the racing and breeding scene in Britain and, as it has spread to their native Dubai and beyond, virtually the world. In this way John Dunlop has left an indelible imprint on the Turf worldwide.

My last professional link with horse racing was severed on 31 December 2009 when I resigned as a non-executive director of Goodwood Racecourse. I considered that a geriatric director was not conducive to a dynamic image of racing at Goodwood. No doubt compulsory retirement would have followed soon if I had not acted, but I thought it was better to forestall it. In my thirty-two years on the Board I had known only two chairmen, the Earl of March who became the tenth Duke of Richmond on the death of his father in 1989, and his son the Earl of March. Neither of them had given any indication of a desire to get rid of me, but I could not count on their indulgence for ever.

While continuing the family tradition of chairmanship of the horse racing company, the younger Earl of March had inherited his grandfather's passion for the motor car and channelled it into founding two major motor events, the Festival of Speed in July and the Revival Meeting in September. Both were hugely successful, attracted vast crowds and raised Goodwood to an unprecedented height of popular recognition. But these events were really beyond my ken.

Index